ABOVE OUR HEADS

Copyright © 1999 by Spencer C. Gibbs
All rights reserved. Printed in the U.S.A.
First Edition

No part of this publication may be reproduced or transmitted in any form or by any means, electronic or mechanical, including photocopying, recording, or any information storage and retrieval system now known or to be invented, without permission in writing from the publisher, except by a reviewer who wishes to quote brief passages in connection with a review written for inclusion in a magazine, newspaper or broadcast.

All photographs contained herein and the college seal are used with the express permission of Morehouse College.

Printed by The Hunt Printing Company, New York City.

Published by Hamilton House Publishers, Ltd.,
3 Hamilton Terrace, New York, NY 10031
www.readwritebooks.com

Library of Congress Catalog Card Number: 00-133794

ISBN: 0-9703276-0-9

The Making of a Morehouse Man

Dedicated to my grandmother, Minnie Harris Gibbs
and my parents, William and Eththelle Gibbs,
for pointing the way.

ABOVE OUR HEADS

Acknowledgments

From the dedication it is obvious the importance that my grandmother Minnie Harris Gibbs (Morris College, Class of 1923) had in leading me to choose Morehouse. Certainly none of this would have been possible without her timely and wise advice. My parents' incredibly enormous contribution lay in the fact that they continue to be inveterate pack rats. Both children of the Depression, they saved the letters that provided the basis for my ruminations, having no idea that there would ever exist a purpose that would lead to their resurrection from the closet in which they sat for over twenty years.

During the preparation of this book I received invaluable assistance from a number of good friends. I would like to thank my classmate Michael Holmes for reading my first attempts at developing a manuscript. His encouragement led me to believe that this was a worthwhile project beyond simply what I had believed. Cliff Flanders, a colleague, friend and fellow Presbyterian, gave critical attention to the manuscript when it was in its earliest stage and provided valuable input as to necessary grammatical and syntactical alterations. Another friend and fraternity brother, J. Roi Jones from law school days, read the entire manuscript while traveling to The Gambia and was so impressed by my efforts that it was humbling. J. Andre Penix Smith, editor of the *Afro Times* (New York City), lent her professional expertise by editing the entire manuscript and giving a number of tips for improving the overall presentation. Victor Wright, my Pi chapter brother, did a great deal to encourage me during the early days of the project before a manuscript had been fully developed. LaVerne M. Cave,

Esq. resolved a number of legal concerns and raised important marketing issues which helped to get the book before the public. Both of my brothers, Marvin and Billy, who also were students at Morehouse, gave constant support and grew as excited as I as the book neared completion. Pearl Griffin of Morehouse College was helpful in allowing me to obtain the permission to use the photographs which are found throughout the book and on the cover. Rev. M. William Howard, a colleague and friend throughout the years, provided me with wonderful anecdotes from his memories of our time together at the 'House.

Finally, I would like to extend a special word of thanks to Mr. Leonard Stevens, the president of The Hunt Printing Company for his support and friendship as well as printing the book you hold. It was Brother Stevens, a long-time member of the Mt. Morris Ascension Presbyterian Church and one of the few Black printers in America willing to take on a book project such as mine, who alerted me to the local publishing netwok that led to my forming Hamilton House Publishers, Ltd. He and his hard-working staff, especially René, André and Rod, were all extremely accomodating to my often anxious demeanor.

The Making of a Morehouse Man

Foreword

Since my second semester at Morehouse College I have always considered myself a Morehouse Man. Why? Because I went through (graduated from) Morehouse, and Morehouse went through me.

At age 12 or 13, when I was first introduced to Dr. Benjamin E. Mays (he was the featured speaker at the New York State Beauty Culturists annual luncheon), I was touched by the African Holy Ghost power that emanated from this epitome of integrity. Dr. Mays was the "Morehouse Man." Speaking without notes, as if the majesty of wind, ocean and fire found vocal expression in his oration, he changed my life forever. It was not only his speaking. It was him. His appearance, neat, not pretentious, yet stylish. His manner, polite and charming, yet strong and fearless. His grace was disarming, and camouflaged a subtle arrogance that said without words: "You know and I know that I'm good, very good." This was Morehouse.

I wanted to be like Dr. Mays! I buried this in a secret chamber of my heart, and went on with my years as a teenager. It was not until my mother suggested that I apply to Morehouse College (limited finances prevented me from attending a small Ivy League college in Connecticut), that the smoldering ember of Dr. Mays' spirit began to break forth "like a fire shut up in my bones." My mother had been touched by the power that came from Dr. Mays. She said that she had heard him speak while she was a student at Georgia State College in Savannah. "If I ever have a son," she said after seeing and hearing Benjamin E. Mays speak, "I would like him to be like Dr. Mays." As circumstances would have it, I enrolled. Only mildly enthusiastic, I recall thinking to myself: If after one year at Morehouse my grades were "A's," I could transfer to the other school with a full scholarship. After my first semester at Morehouse, I completely forgot about the college in Connecticut.

When I arrived in Atlanta in August of 1967, Dr. Mays had retired. Dr. Hugh Morris Gloster was soon to be inaugurated the eighth president of Morehouse College. I was heart-broken. Who is this man? I wanted Benjamin E. Mays. He was the real "Morehouse Man." My brief disappointment would soon disappear as this gravel-voiced Morehouse Man began to place his own indelible mark on the college and the students who studied under his leadership. Dr. Gloster became MY PRESIDENT in the spirit of the Morehouse bond.

Yet, how was this possible? No Dr. Mays, then there could be no Morehouse. It was this change in leadership that helped me to see that Morehouse is more than Dr. Benjamin E. Mays. Morehouse College is a mystical union of spirit, intellect and personality rooted in the history of a racist America, comprised of strong college presidents, talented, dynamic, committed, sacrificial faculty, and unique men who, in the crucible of academic rigor, positive peer pressure and constant reminders that we were being trained to rebel and serve, were bound together "... in ties more brotherly."

Part of my elementary education was received in Corona, Queens, New York. There was a teacher to whose class I was never assigned. Mrs. Jackson was one of only two Black teachers in the school. She lived in our community, went to church in our community, she was part of us. She would often say to me,

The Making of a Morehouse Man

"You're smart, but I need you in my class." I did not quite understand as a fourth, fifth, and sixth grader, but I could feel that I was missing something not having her as a teacher. It was not academic. It was something far more important.

I had never been to a homecoming game before 1967 or seen two Black college football teams engaged in what seemed to be mortal combat. So many cordial Black folk, so many pretty, brown-skinned women on one small piece of land. More than these things, to see and hear a chorus of Black men sing a song with such force that it shook the very foundation of my being, "Lift every voice and sing..." Tears ran down my face like sheets of water cascading over a fall. I felt the earth shake beneath me. I was on Holy ground. It was hallowed by Mordecai Johnson, Howard Thurman, Benjamin Mays, Martin L. King, Jr, and countless more whose names, while not familiar to many, gave of themselves to serve "the least of these" under the ever-present shadow of our "alma mater." Oh! Mrs. Jackson! I was finally in your class. The academics were there but that was not what I was missing; it was far more important than that. It was my soul. I found me.

As only a true son of Morehouse can, Spencer Gibbs tells the story of the personal pride and pain in the making of a Morehouse Man. By revealing himself, Gibbs provides the reader with one authentic look into the Morehouse Mystique, and why Morehouse, Tuskeegee, Howard, Spelman, Claflin, Dillard, Fisk, Xavier, et. alia, still provide excellent venues for building the content of our character.

Calvin O. Butts, '71
Abyssinian, New York City
July 4, 2000

The Making of a Morehouse Man

Prologue

Before my senior year of high school, I had not heard of Morehouse College. This is especially embarrassing to admit as my paternal grandparents, my mother, her sisters and brothers, and my father's sisters had all been educated in African-American colleges in the South. It was not until I was nearing the threshold of graduation that my grandmother had a chat with me about my college plans. She asked simply: "Have you considered attending a Negro college?" This caught me totally off guard.

As I stood there pondering a response that would not reveal my complete ignorance, or worse, my bias, she put another question in my way: "Have you ever heard of Morehouse College? It's an all-male college for Negroes. Why don't you go for a year and then, if you don't like it, you can always transfer to a white school?"

It was as though she were reading my mind before I could formulate the thoughts. Up until this time I had gone to predominately white schools. It had never occurred to me to apply to a Black college. Like so many Black students of that time, attendance at a Black college was thought to be settling for less. In fact, in my high school graduating class, all but one other than myself had already decided upon the white school they would be attending in the coming September. My grandmother appeared, though, to have had some special insight that had been kept hidden from me until now. It dawned on me almost instantly that her suggestion made all the sense in the world. I began to wonder about all of the other times she had offered advice that I

The Making of a Morehouse Man

ignored because I thought she just did not understand my concerns.

Immediately, I wanted to know everything, all at once, about this place called Morehouse. An all-male college for Black men? Where was it? Who were its alumni? Why hadn't I been told about it before now? She patiently answered all of my questions, excited over my enthusiasm. And her answers fueled my drive to learn more. I began to ask other people, particularly Black students in my high school class, about Morehouse. Hardly anyone had heard of it. During this time, the publicity surrounding the man who was soon to become its most famous alumnus did not link Dr. Martin Luther King, Jr. to his alma mater. This demonstrated how little information was circulated about the school and how small its importance was perceived to be by the larger society.

When I received my letter of acceptance on May 6, 1965, all of the other college options that I was entertaining became no options at all. By this time I had talked with a few men who had gone there or knew of persons who had. None of them had anything but the most superlative comments to make about their experiences there. Some spoke in almost reverential tones, so thankful were they to have had the opportunity to spend their formative years at Morehouse.

The college was founded in 1867, in Augusta, Georgia as the Augusta Institute by the Rev. William Jefferson White with the financial support of the American Baptist Home Mission Society. The institute was first housed in the basement of the Springfield Baptist Church. Rev. White, though he looked like a white man, was the offspring of a white father and Native American mother. He later married a Black woman, became an ordained Baptist minister and pastored the African-American congregation of Augusta's Springfield Baptist Church. With such an uncommon man as its founder, it is little wonder that the school survived its early years and flourished in later ones.

In 1879, the Rev. Frank Quarles, pastor of Friendship Baptist Church in Atlanta, persuaded the school's leaders to move the campus to Atlanta. It was then housed in the basement of Friendship and in 1913, the name was changed to Morehouse College in honor of Henry L. Morehouse, corresponding secretary of the American Baptist Home Mission Society. It was not until 1906, that the college was to have its first African-American president in the person of John Hope, who established the direction and corporate culture of the school that was to be followed for the next 40 years. It was President Hope who instilled the pride in Morehouse reflected by its graduates and students today.

Upon entering into the cloistered community of Morehouse in 1965, I learned that the total student body had reached its highest enrollment ever with less than 900. Since its founding, there had been only 3,200 graduates. Nineteen alumni had served or were currently serving as college presidents. One of every eight graduates possessed either an academic or professional doctorate. Of the 65 members of the faculty, 53% held doctorates (from 1967 statistical data). Forty-five of these faculty members were African-Americans and 23 of them held the highest degree in their fields. This fact alone had enormous impact upon me. All during my primary and secondary school experiences, I had never received formal classroom instruction from a Black teacher. Now I was being taught not just by Black people, but Black professors with Ph.Ds. The significance of this has

ABOVE OUR HEADS:

THE MAKING OF A MOREHOUSE MAN

by
SPENCER C. GIBBS '69

HAMILTON HOUSE PUBLISHERS, LTD.
new york city

The Making of a Morehouse Man

many layers.

They were at once demanding and compassionate. We were challenged not just by rigorous classroom instruction, but also by the example of their own accomplishments. Some of the faculty had graduated from Morehouse and felt strongly that they had a legacy of excellence they were duty-bound to convey through their teaching and behavior. We almost had the feeling of being junior colleagues to these teachers because they absolutely believed in our abilities and were committed to helping us fulfill our academic as well as personal goals for advancement. Many of the faculty without doctorates were pursuing them even while carrying a full teaching load. This, too, had the effect of causing us to believe that there were no limits to what we might be able to achieve.

During July Fourth, 1992, I visited with my parents. One afternoon my father came into the den where I was talking with my son Christian and handed me an old cardboard box, announcing it contained some papers I might find interesting. When I opened the box and began inspecting its contents, I could not believe my eyes. In that box were all the letters I had written my parents during my four years as a student at Morehouse. After reading a few of them, the memories of those days flooded my mind. Then it occurred to me that these letters might form the basis of a book. In recent times I had begun asking myself: What was it about this college that produced such qualitative graduates? I wondered, too, if anyone else was pondering this or cared. I had read articles about Morehouse in *Essence* magazine, *U.S News and World Report*, *The Wall Street Journal* and other periodicals so I knew Morehouse was at least newsworthy. Yet, none of these pieces were written with an insider's passion that made the school come alive for me in the way I had experienced it.

This book, however, is not intended to be "a history of Morehouse" such as the detailed and authoritative account entitled *A Candle in the Dark*, written by my former French professor, Dr. Edward A. Jones, a 1926 graduate of the college. Rather, what I have attempted here are personal reflections that explore the individual and communal influences that shaped the lives of those who attended this wondrous place.

I have not sought to correct the grammar or syntactical errors replete throughout the letters written to my parents that begin each chapter, hoping that in their original form they would better convey the spirit of the moment in which they were written. It is my wish that college brothers of mine who spent the four or more years it takes to receive a degree from "The 'House," as Morehouse is referred to by those who attended, will read these musings with fond memories and a renewed appreciation for the college that trained them to lead. I hope that readers who did not go to Morehouse will come to understand why it is one of the greatest liberal arts colleges in this country and why for the bulk of its existence it has been content to attract, to borrow from a popular recruiting slogan, a few good men. More importantly, it is my prayer that readers will come to realize how a place with such meager financial resources for the bulk of its more than 130 years, in an environment hostile to its mission of educating and building Black men, could have enjoyed such an immense measure of success. Howard Thurman, the noted religious thinker, Christian mystic and graduate of the class of 1923, wrote these words from which the title of this book was inspired:

The Making of a Morehouse Man

"Over the heads of her students, Morehouse holds a crown that she challenges them to grow tall enough to wear."

>Spencer C. Gibbs, '69
>New York City, 1999

The Making of a Morehouse Man

YEAR ONE

The Year of the Crab

"Morehouse College, Morehouse College
Morehouse College bless her name.
Whether in defeat or victory,
We are loyal just the same.

"And we'll cheer for Morehouse College
'Tis for her we'll fight for fame.
And we'll sing her praises loud in every land,
Morehouse College, bless her name."

The Morehouse College Fight Song

The Making of a Morehouse Man

1

Monday, Sept. 6, 1965

Dear Folks,

I arrived in Atlanta at 11:30 AM Saturday morning. The activities for that day consisted of securing quarters and luggage, a simple task theoretically but difficult in practice. This is the largest freshman class Morehouse has had and there was much confusion that day.

My roommate is an Alaskan can you get that? Out of some 387 freshies I have the only Alaskan student. He's a good guy though and pretty bright, I guess. He was second in his class but the class only consisted of seven people.

We at Morehouse have quite an appetite for study and books. So if I don't do well it's not because I didn't study but because I am not smart enough.

Everybody here are good people, real chums. The freshmen are known as "crabs" as in crabgrass and must state their name as "Crab Gibbs," in my case, whenever asked by an upper classman.

All this week we have tests which are supposed to be quite trying to the intelligence of Morehouse freshies. These tests will determine our level of learning and our rank in class.

Spelman girls come Tuesday. Nobody cares, however, because we know they already admire us

Above Our Heads

(Morehouse Men).
 If you have any questions about the "House" don't hesitate. I'm finding out something everyday. Will right (sic) soon.

Love,
Spencer

Address: Spencer Gibbs
Rm 208 Bldg. 5
Quarles Court
Morehouse College
Atlanta, Georgia 30314

As I was standing on the platform at Union Station waiting with my parents to board the L & N Railroad train to Atlanta, I could not contain my excitement. In a few minutes not only was I going to be emancipated from my parents' protective grasp, but I was soon to be on my greatest adventure. This was the first and longest train trip I had taken without a family member to a destination that was wholly unfamiliar. Though I had talked with people about Morehouse, even looking at class yearbooks that captured scenes of campus life, I realized I was still going to a mysterious place. As it turned out, my father struck up a conversation with another man who was sending his son to college. Seconds later I was introducing myself to Duane Jackson and his friend, Robert Cross, both enrolling as freshmen at Morehouse.
 Before the train trip was over we three had become fast friends.

The Making of a Morehouse Man

Like me, they had been born in Chicago and had lived there all their lives. Unlike me, they were the sons of Morehouse graduates. As we talked, they revealed to me that as far back as they could remember they knew they were going to attend their fathers' college. It was clear. They were raised to believe that there was no other choice: they were going to go to college and the college was going to be Morehouse. I began to imagine that they had been brainwashed, for they did not show the slightest bit of resentment towards what I perceived to be coercion on the part of their fathers. The more we talked, however, the more I sensed from them a genuine desire to want to go to school at Morehouse. It was mildly eerie, I remembered thinking, yet, by the time we arrived in Atlanta, I believe I had decided that if I had a son, he too would be educated there.

Upon first seeing the campus, I was crestfallen. Indeed, I had not been prepared for what I saw. It had rained the day before and the red clay of Georgia had become saturated and flowed out upon the street, sidewalk and seemingly everywhere. You couldn't walk without stepping in its gooey residue. Passing cars would splash it upon the lower portions of buildings which had the effect of making the well-worn campus structures look even more neglected than they were. Soon, however, these feelings passed and I found myself quickly getting caught up in the energy of my new home. Anyway, Bob and Duane, who had visited the campus on occasion with their fathers, helped me to shrug off my depression with their unbridled excitement at having finally made it to "The 'House."

After waiting in interminable lines to be assigned housing, I was finally able to secure a room key and join a couple of other fellows who were lodging in the same quarters. I was to live on the top floor of a two-story building in a small five-building housing complex called Quarles Court. Each of the buildings, known as The Units, were identical, containing ten rooms, each to be shared by two students. One additional larger room on the second floor was to be shared by as many as four, and a second room identical to it directly under it was to be used as the lounge. There were no amenities, but the simplest of furnishings: a set of bunk beds, a desk with work stations on opposing sides and two chairs. The desk was designed to accommodate simultaneously the study needs of two students, but I rarely saw it used in that way. Most persons usually studied in the library or in the room when the other was not present.

As students began to fill up the rooms in Unit 5, I began to meet guys from places I had only heard about and some places I never knew to exist. There was Clarence Yokely from High Point, North Carolina. He liked to remark from time to time that High Point was the "Sprinklerhead Capital" of the world. A tall, lanky guy from Sheffield, Alabama named Robert Goldston and his roommate Billy Gilbert, from Monroe, Louisiana, became the dorm comics. Ever since its beginning, Morehouse has had a student body predominately comprised of Southerners from Georgia, Alabama and Florida. By the time that I got there, the school liked to boast that it attracted students from every state in the union and a number of foreign countries. While that claim is certainly true today, it was more a goal to be reached in the Sixties. Morehouse then was still essentially a regional school with a handful of students from places such as Chicago, New York City and California. The stereotypes about the quality of south-

The Making of a Morehouse Man

ern Black educational institutions were reflected in the dearth of students hailing from states outside the South.

In time the unit had its full complement of residents save one: my roommate. Quite a lot of time expired waiting for this guy to finally arrive. The other fellows began making jokes, speculating about who my roommate would be. I'm sure I overheard someone make the crack that my roommate would probably be a white guy. In my mind this played a cruel irony as I began to anticipate the occurrence of such an event. One of the reasons I chose Morehouse was because I wanted to experience a Black educational environment. Nevertheless, the school had attracted one or two white fellows every so often, therefore my having a white roommate became a very real possibility. Then, as soon as I began contemplating my reaction to this, standing in the doorway of my room was what appeared to be a young Indian fellow asking me if this was Room 208, Unit 5. I cringed as I begrudgingly answered in the affirmative.

Nick was an Inuit, an Eskimo from Alaska. After living with him for a semester, this was, regrettably, about as much as I ever learned about him. Looking back on that time, it's difficult now to have to accept that I was as shallow as I was toward people with whom I had little familiarity. Sadly, this was true of many in my unit and throughout the student body. He was ostracized and treated shabbily by my classmates and myself. Through no fault of his own, Nick simply failed to fit our understanding of the profile of the student who was to attend Morehouse. Because of the severity of student response to him, within the semester Nick had suffered a nervous breakdown and was forced to leave the college. Before he left, but after it was too late to reverse the damage, there was an overwhelming sense of remorse experienced by all of us who had never taken the time to address our prejudice as evidenced by the way we treated Nick. My mind will not allow me to release this memory. For I saw firsthand the evil power of unwarranted bias and fear. I resolved then, as did some of my classmates, that this kind of race hate or cultural superiority was, for us, going to be unacceptable behavior in which we would not knowingly participate.

Yet the treatment received by Nick was to a much lesser extent meted out to others in our cloistered enclave. Since the dominant group consisted of rural southerners, those of us who hailed from other social strata were considered suspicious until we were adjudged to be regular guys. Therefore, if you were a Chicagoan like me, you would learn to survive by being able to "take" the abusive joking about your speech patterns, for example. Quickly, one learned how not to make references to one's northern cultural upbringing and experiences that might be in any way interpreted to sound as though you were better than your southern counterpart. Indeed, if you had half a brain at all, you came to see that the west and south sides of Chicago and Harlem were actually "Up South"; that Southerners were you and you were them.

Freshman Week, the first seven days of the Morehouse freshman's life, is spent learning about the customs and traditions of the school. Not just to prepare you for the psychological rigors of the classroom but, as importantly, for life with the upperclassmen. One of the facts learned early on is that we were Crabs - first year students with no academic credits to our name. A "Morehouse Man," which we all mistakenly assumed we were with acceptance to the school, was one who had survived the first semester as evidenced by having amassed "hours" in the registrar's office, that is, completed a semester's course work.

Even though we were the lowest students on the Morehouse totem, we were amazed somewhat to learn that our upperclass brothers regarded us more highly than they did the upperclass students at any of the other colleges in the Atlanta University Center. The AUC consisted of Morehouse; Spelman College, a women's undergraduate college; two coeducational undergrad schools, Morris Brown and Clark College; a graduate school, Atlanta University; and six divinity schools that comprised the Interdenominational Theological Center. The interesting phenomenon that we observed as time went on was that the students in these other schools, except for the Spelman women, seemed to view us with envy. Of course, one would be hard-pressed to prove this, but soon we began hearing the axiom, "you can always tell a Morehouse Man, but you can't tell him much." We never heard a similar expression applied to students from the other Atlanta schools.

At the same time we were experiencing Freshman Week, so too were the Spelman students. We were not allowed by our upperclass mentors to have any contact with them until the fifth day of the week and then only in a controlled environment. Before laying eyes upon these women, I had never before seen so many consistently beautiful young ladies in one place in all my life. I began mentally thanking my grandmother for all of my apparent good fortune.

Before that first meeting, Morehouse students had been matched with a Spelman student, without the knowledge of

Above Our Heads

either, for the dance that would celebrate the end of Freshman Week. In retrospect, this seems archaic and perhaps even unjust: for while Morehouse students had very little to complain about in this arrangement, Spelman students were often not so fortunate. The dance occurred prior to the return of the upper classes; we were, therefore, able to meet the newest class of Spelman ladies before our older brothers could. We thought that we had the upper hand. This could not have been further from the truth. Only under the rarest circumstances did the budding romances between Morehouse and Spelman freshmen survive beyond the first month. Upon the return of the upperclassmen, Spelman students were quickly swept away by them and we were left to languish.

In contrast to Morehouse, Spelman's grounds were like the vast, well-manicured lawns of some enormously wealthy land baron. And this impression was not altogether inaccurate. Spelman College was named for Laura Spelman Rockefeller and the wealth of the Rockefeller family was self-evident in the buildings and well-designed, tree-lined, park-like setting that was its campus. This was going to be the beginning of the best time of my life.

The Making of a Morehouse Man

2

Sept. 21, 1965

Dear Mom & Dad,

I have forty minutes until my next class which is a social science lecture. In your last letter you requested a schedule of my classes. Here it is:

```
         MON      TUES     WED     THUR    FRI     SAT

 8:00             Math             Math            Math
 9:00    Chapel            Chapel          Chapel
 9:40
10:40    English           English         English
11:40    French            French   Frosh  French  Hum.
                                    Lecture Lecture
12:30    Lunch ─────────────────────────────────────────
 1:45    Social   Personal  Soc     Pers.          Soc.
         Science  Living    Sci     Liv.           Sci.
 2:45    Physical Humanities Phys.          Humanities
         Educ.              Educ.
```

All the other hours are used, in my case for study (really!). Refer to the catalogue if you want an explanation of courses.

Mom are you working on Ph. D. at University of Chicago yet? I am having difficulty getting adjusted to classroom activities. I guess this is because the spirit of competition is so great. I am taking steps to overcome this but I am not ashamed to say I'm afraid of my suc-

Above Our Heads

cess at Morehouse. The faculty is so great —- 36 doctorates, 62 teachers and they give us lots of work. I am trying my best to stay in and realize that if I don't it's not cause I'm not working. Morehouse drops half of the freshman class after the first term. This statistic is enough to make me work my hardest.

The campus is very academically-minded yet there is a degree of socializing with the other colleges in the area as well. I talked to several students and they feel that a person with 3 A's and 2 B's for example is really nothing spectacular. I'm hoping for at least a B-average but find that I will have to work at a tremendous pace to attain it.

I hope you don't hate me if I get some C's the first time. I just must get used to the work here.

When should I call home or should I?

Out of a total of $103 - excluding the train fair I've spent $89.83. Here is where the money went:

Frosh Orientation	17.00
Baggage Fee (delivered to Morehouse)	2.00
Treat	1.55
Dinner that Sunday upon arriving	1.30
Train expenses	3.30
Key deposit	2.00
1 Crab hat	2.06
1 spt. shirt	2.04
2 pr. wash pants	14.09
(no laundry service for first month)	
1 snack	.74
3 shirts (laundered)	.43
Set of books (used)	25.19

The Making of a Morehouse Man

1 book (new)	6.13
2 book (used)	4.00
Miss. (numerous small items)	8.00
	89.33
Balance approx. $13—	

Love,
Spencer

After the first week, more than 100 members of the class did not return. I understood this. It seemed that everyone in my class, except myself, had graduated first or second in his class. Everyone had been accepted to a variety of colleges other than Morehouse. I remember having a conversation among five or six of us and learning that all of them had been accepted to at least one Ivy League college and a couple had been nominated and received appointments to two of the service academies. After the first week, we really still did not know fully what to expect during the coming year, but one thing was clear: this was not going to be a cakewalk. Many of the guys who were accepted to more prestigious schools had agreed to come to Morehouse for Freshman Week and if they didn't like what they saw, would accept an admission offer elsewhere. This accounted for a number of students leaving. Their attitude was that if we're going to work so hard, why not get an Ivy-covered degree.

I was staying regardless of that first week's experience, which, remarkably, was incredibly positive. Of 253 men who began the first year in earnest, I had an unbelievable ranking of 19 based on the placement examinations given and my scores from the stan-

Above Our Heads

dard college entrance examination. But equally important, I really liked the place! I felt a part of something special.

The Spelman women were absolutely the most beautiful women on the planet. For the first time in my life I actually began to believe that I could attract one of them. It was this Morehouse thing: as though the world were opening up for me simply because I had been fortunate enough to go to college there. I'm sure that these early feelings of confidence were nurtured and fueled by the rarefied atmosphere created by so many self-assured, young, talented Black men feeding on one another's positive energy.

I was running scared the first few days of the year once the routine grind of classwork began. I was taking a full load, 18 hours. The rationale was to become so immersed in study that I would not have time to mess about. It did not quite work out that way. I had an absolute ball my first year! Somehow I discovered that I was able to party late and still make an 8:00 a. m. math class on Saturday. I began to believe I was smarter than I had remembered myself to be in high school. It was the place - the combination of the student body and the faculty. Everybody there was bright. Some were truly exceptional, but everyone seemed gifted. Each of us had a vision for our future and could articulate it. This may have not been true before we came to Morehouse but it certainly came to be so during that very first week. Perhaps it was the peer pressure forcing us to take our futures seriously. It definitely was the school's agenda to cause us to develop this way of thinking. The instructors encouraged this as well, pushing us to see the relationship between understanding the learnings of Humanities I, for example, and a career in medicine. From as far back as elementary school, I remember being taught that school was the place where one learned to assimilate into the society or, put another way, to know the responsibilities of citizenship. In high school we learned that school was there to teach one how to think. I was to learn that Morehouse's mission was to teach men how to lead.

3

Sept. 27, 1965

Dear Folks,

    So far I have had no tests and am unable to tell you of my progress relating to grades. The weather here is getting colder and I would appreciate it if you would send my coat down at your convenience.

    How are Marvin and Billy? There are a couple of fellows here by that name Marvin and a great deal named Billy? I hope they're not getting into very much trouble.

    I'm going to be a Morehouse cheerleader for the football and possibly basketball season. I think that this will enable me to attend away games free of charge. I think that I will still have enough time to study; I've worked out a pretty adequate schedule.

    I just came from chapel and once again I was given some advice by Mr. William Nix, placement director, on getting your studies. So I immediately went to my room and started studying my French. When I did this, however, I remembered that I hadn't written in a week. Things on campus are so trivial, with the exception of academics, that there is really nothing to write about.

    Just like you said Daddy the fellows here on campus are able to obtain beer or liquor and on the weekends drink quite a lot. I admit that I have once but don't by any means intend to make a habit of it.

    The surrounding schools give parties quite frequently but are usually attended by Morehouse students. I have limited myself, however, to the weekend (they party on weekdays at Clark College) and then only on Saturday possibly Friday night.

That's all I can think of for now. I'm doing better, I think, in Dr. Hume's English class but the work is coming in stronger every day.

Love,
Spencer

I had my first drink of hard liquor with George Watson on the rear porch of Unit 5. George bought a half-pint of Hiram Walker and we told each other lies the rest of the night. He was from Nyack, New York near the Tappan Zee Bridge. He made it sound closer to New York City than it actually was. We became good buddies during the year, but everyone living in Unit 5 became close. The architectural scale of the residence encouraged community-building. Morehouse tended to be comprised of several communities of students that were developed in accordance with dorm life. During the first year, freshmen were segregated from the larger student body in terms of living quarters and coursework. Afterwards, student networks transcended class year and residence hall. Class distinctions were not as sharply defined for those in the upper classes. After all, these people had secured the coveted "Morehouse Man" status. Years later this designation was only to apply to her graduates.

Freshmen, though generally affirmed by the college, were, nevertheless, Crabs. As such, we had to respond to the wishes of upperclassmen by acceding to their demands for service. These usually amounted to running some errand or being turned into a

Above Our Heads

laughingstock for the enjoyment of the taunting sophomore or junior. Seniors were above this sort of hazing as they were consumed with graduating and moving on to the next steps toward graduate and professional school or their career. Yet, the abuse of Crabs was seen as great fun by those upperclassmen who participated in it and enormously demeaning for those victimized by it.

I was walking to Yates and Milton, a corner drugstore and extremely popular campus hangout at the intersection of what was then Chestnut and Fair streets. On a low-rise brick bearing wall that delineated the northeastern corner of the Morehouse campus sat about six upperclassmen who were just waiting for some hapless Crab to humiliate. One of the guys barked at me to come where they were sitting. He looked at me and then began to ask who I was. After giving my name and identifying myself as a freshman, he corrected me by instructing me that I will always refer to myself as "Crab Gibbs" and I'd be well-advised not to forget it or something unsavory would occur to me. I thought this type of threat was going a bit far, so I started to walk away. I got six inches when he began to chide me for my dialect which was clearly northern and not reflective of his Alabama background. By this time I was starting to become a little nervous because the other guys were now beginning to take an interest in what was going on and started their own round of questioning, interspersed with laughter and threats, now that my northern background was exposed.

The principal antagonist, becoming annoyed or bored, dismissed me by ordering me to go across the street to the store and purchase him a pack of cigarettes. Thankful to be released, I walked across the street, towards Yates and Milton...and passed it.

The Making of a Morehouse Man

I decided that there were much better things to do that afternoon than visiting Y & M. I kept walking faster and faster until I was running, intent upon placing as much distance between them and myself as I could. I only hoped that when I did see this guy again he would have forgotten me. As it turned out, he did but I did not. I had always believed that bullying was obnoxious and unwarranted behavior, but this victimization caused me to begin to formulate in my mind ways of challenging it when I saw it. I also made up my mind that I would not participate in crab-hazing if I returned for a second year.

In the case of the bullying upperclassman, justice was ultimately served. Instead of graduating with his class in 1967, he did not receive a degree until two years after I received mine. He ended up becoming a patrolman with the Atlanta Police Department, which somehow seemed a profession consistent with his earlier behavior.

I believed that I was too small to play football for the Tigers, so I thought that I would become a cheerleader instead. This way I could go to all of the away games without expense and enjoy the true benefits that came with Morehouse cheerleading: getting to know the Spelman women who were also cheerleaders for Morehouse. While cheerleading was for many of us viewed as a woman's thing to do, attendance at an all-male college challenged my perception of this, but not enough. When I finally weighed the benefits (free trips to games, socializing with the female cheerleaders) against the liabilities (long hours of practice, mandatory attendance at every game, not being able to sit in the bleachers with your buddies), I decided against it. Later, after watching the cheerleading squad at games, I began mildly to regret my decision. They seemed to be having so much fun.

When Samuel L. Jackson, the present-day film star, entered Morehouse in my second year, he and his crew seemed to elevate cheerleading to an unprecedented level of popularity when he tried out for the squad, was accepted and became its most popular cheerleader. It was a feeling close to envy to watch these male cheerleaders, as they decided that they would not actually do the cheers, they would simply stand and strike macho type poses and let the women jump up and down assisting only when a routine appropriately called for an "escort." The crowd loved it and Samuel L. Jackson, as Morehouse cheerleader, became an archetype for "cool."

Freshman chapel was mandatory at this time and proved to be informative if not entertaining. It was in chapel where I was exposed to the critical thinkers of the day. I remember vividly the appearances of Dr. Howard Thurman and Dr. Martin Luther King, Jr. as chapel speakers. It was here that the Morehouse community received its philosophical and moral foundation. Yet, chapel was far more than a forum for the dissemination of religious ideology. We heard talks on etiquette and the way that a proper gentleman moves about in a civilized society. We were being equipped for balancing the demands of a life in the boardroom as well as the bedroom. I recall one session in which a sexologist lectured on the most effective way of erotically stimulating a woman. On this particular occasion there were a few Spelman women present. The speaker seemed to delight in going into great detail about how a man massages a woman and engages in foreplay. This had the effect of simultaneously embarrassing those of us who sat near the women and arousing them.

The Making of a Morehouse Man

A friend remarked to me not long ago that chapel was the place where he first heard the music of Miles Davis as part of a music appreciation lecture delivered by Dr. Willis Lawrence James, venerated chairman of the Morehouse Music Department until 1965.

We were taught lessons about dining and drinking. The school was big on making the point that if you are in the public eye, you should know the correct manner in which to carry yourself. There was also another reason for why proper social mores were taught. Many of the students who attended Morehouse at this time were from communities so deep in the backwoods of Georgia and Alabama that the towns in which they grew up did not have restaurants. These students, then, had had no opportunity to learn or experience formal dining or dining in a public setting. Therefore, students were lectured on the proper way to hold a fork, to cut a piece of steak, to refrain from sopping one's gravy (a tough lesson to practice) and many other nuances of civilized dining that were designed to add polish and poise to a gentleman.

The college took seriously its role of training men for leadership. This included what many may have considered the mundane instruction of teaching proper social graces. The school's most ardent proponent of this position was Dr. Brailsford Reese Brazeal, dean of the college.

This man was at once perceived as brilliant and a buffoon. He was educated at Morehouse and Columbia University, receiving both a master's degree and doctorate from the latter. A member of the Morehouse Class of 1927, he was the 14th alumnus in the history of the college to be awarded a Ph.D., which he received in 1942, no easy feat in any age. Yet, notwithstanding his enormously impressive credentials, his speech belied his deep southern rural roots and it sounded as if he had a mouth full of marbles whenever he spoke. He was known less for earth-shaking gems of wisdom and more for his extremely elementary and idiosyncratic style of communication that tended, unfortunately, to make him a laughingstock. For example, he had a habit of spelling words out as a way of underscoring a point even though emphasis was not needed. One day Dean Brazeal was instructing that a gentleman always brings flowers when collecting a lady at her door for an evening date. One student asked what flowers tended to be most appropriate for this occasion. He remarked, "chrysanthemums, c-h-r... Er, ah, roses. Roses would be good, r-o-s-e-s, roses!"

For Dean Brazeal, chivalry would never die as long as he had anything to do with it. Once he commented on the correct way to walk with a woman on a public way.

"Always walk on the side of the lady nearer the street." A student asked what should a man do when there is no street and the sidewalk runs between parallel rows of buildings.

Obviously frustrated and following an uncomfortably long pause the dean spurted out, "You can walk on her right, her left, behind her or in front of her, wherever you want."

After a lengthy period of laughter subsided, I had to wonder why it seemed that through all of this Dean Brazeal appeared never to be embarrassed. I'll never forget that it was the Dean who first instructed us that we should never slice our meat entree in many pieces all at once; only slice off the piece you intend to put in your mouth at the moment. Some lessons you never forget and that is one I recall almost every time I sit down to a meal.

4

October 6, 1965

Dear Parents,

    I just came from Math class and received my first test paper back, an "A." I'm feeling very good right now with the idea that I'm going to keep up the good work. There is a place directly north (across the street) from school known as The Canterbury House. This is a place sponsored by the Episcopal Church where students may come and study and engage in intellectual conversation. Right behind the Canterbury House is a smaller residential house (four rooms) where three guys are now living. There (sic) names are Barry Gaither, Charlie Mack, and Haywood Hodge. They take care of the Canterbury establishment and in turn have the opportunity to live in the smaller house with rent deductions. They are seniors at Morehouse. This is where I now am writing this letter.

    I've met a lot of fellows here and get along with everyone. I got out of the cheerleading squad but still have the desires (sic) to go to Howard and Fisk football games. I may join the Glee Club. It's supposed to be the best organization on campus because of its high ideals of brotherhood.

    My roommate and I do not get along very well. It seems that we each have our own friends and are apart from each other. I've tried several times to bring about unity but he resists and then again I'm not very interested.

    You asked about the overcoat's place. It's in the basement in the clear plastic closet near the furnace. I do need those other shirts also, send them at your con-

Above Our Heads

venience.

Duane Jackson and Robert Cross are doing pretty good. Jackson must maintain a "B" average to keep the scholarship he got by his father going to Morehouse.

All the freshmen are close to one another, they each have a common bond, getting through the freshman year. In the next letter I write it will be entirely about these guys.

The girls are in excess. One must use discretion in choosing because there is always a better looking girl. I have become close to four or five different girls (from 16 to 21) and still could learn of more. However, I realize my studies come first and look upon the girls as a luxury when one has nothing else to do but sit around. I am seldom in this state (well at least during the week, I must let loose on the weekends).

When I said before that I was #19 that meant in the entire class. Groups were used in finding out the level you were in: Group I indicated a level of 13 or above, Group II, 10 to 12 grade, Group III, 9th and below. However, (not) much emphasis is placed on this because some of the slow readers are real smart in physics and math.

Five dollars a week is quite sufficient. I realize that if I need more all I have to do is right (sic). Say, I never did receive the box you said you would send me. What happened? This is all for now. Will write at earliest convenience.

                 Love,
                 Your son,
                 Spencer

The Making of a Morehouse Man

When I received that first grade in trigonometry, I felt that there was nothing that would stand in the way of success. Heretofore, I had been a dismal math student and certainly did not see myself heading in the direction of a math or science major. But there was this real sense of triumph that I simply attributed to the climate of learning, competition and the fear of failure. I believe that all of us in the first year were as much afraid of failing in one another's eyes as we were of disappointing our parents and experiencing their wrath. It was this type of peer pressure that had the effect of binding us together while keeping us in competitive tension with one another.

I loved the Canterbury House. It was an informal meeting place where the self-styled literati of the campus community would gather to have impromptu discussions on issues of the day. Meant as a place primarily for Morehouse and Spelman undergraduates, a few students from Clark College and the graduate school, Atlanta University, would occasionally wander in to participate. Canterbury House was a campus ministry of the Episcopal Church and was run by Father Warren Scott who was more on the order of a "Mr. Chips" schoolmaster than an Episcopalian priest.

Father Scott was the first Black priest I had ever met and perhaps the first minister to whom I could relate as another human being. He was completely without pretension and made you feel like the adults the school wanted us to be. I never saw him dressed in anything other than the traditional clerical garb of black clergy shirt and matching black business suit. Yet, he did not possess an inflated sense of his own worth and you saw him as a "regular guy" in the best sense of that expression.

Above Our Heads

Those of us who most often hung out began to take meals with Father Scott. This was a coed group of students who were mainly social science, English, music and art majors. There was Walter Dancy, Michelle Smith, Samuel Ethridge, Arthur Lewis and the guys who lived in the caretaker's cottage behind Canterbury House: Haywood Hodges, Charles Mack and Edmund Barry Gaither. Everyone would have some part to play in the preparation of the meal; from shopping to clean-up. It was such fun and so popular that Fr. Scott had to begin limiting the number of people who could be part of this gathering.

Dinners at Canterbury House were great because you could discuss any subject from school life to world politics. As I mentioned before, this was a place where the campus literary types would mingle. Everyone saw themselves as some kind of Bohemian or at least left-of-center. This was the era in which flower children competed for headlines with the escalating Vietnam War.

"Make Love, Not War" was the nation's campus motto. In my freshman year these coed dinners helped me to understand that there was something terribly intimate about dining with intellectual and beautiful women, even when it was a shared experience with others. Actually, the best of both worlds combined in those moments: one could be socializing with students from Spelman while advancing one's academic purposes. We argued about the pros and cons of the philosophies of Malcolm X over Martin L. King, Jr.; of dedicating oneself to a life of service helping others or simply helping oneself; of the character development of Iago in Shakespeare's Othello, and a vast array of subjects that were generally in the news at that time.

The Making of a Morehouse Man

The bulk of those who met at Canterbury tended to be members of the same college class. While upper classes might socialize there, typically it was a place where freshmen gathered. If one got hooked into its bohemian-like ethos, one might continue into the later years, but generally folks outgrew the Canterbury experience. As freshmen, we naturally looked up to the guys who took care of the place, primarily because they were upperclassmen and had the privilege of living off-campus. Yet, there was also the astonishing fact that they regarded us as peers.

Gaither, Hodge and Mack were also very cool brothers. Barry Gaither was an Art History major with considerable artistic talent. He was headed to a position after graduation as a curator in a prestigious art museum in New York City. Four years of The College had transformed this rural South Carolinian into an extremely knowledgeable man of the world, having been encouraged by his faculty advisor to spend time in travel abroad during summer breaks.

Haywood Hodge from Fort Valley, Georgia appeared to be a philosopher, though he was actually a psychology major. Though Haywood was a sophomore, he simply carried himself with an assurance and confidence characteristic of one much older than he actually was. Maybe the fact that he had a full beard, which at that time was not typical of the Morehouse student, contributed to his unique persona.

If Gaither and Hodge were considered campus Bohemians, then Charlie Mack seemed a holdover from the Fifties' Beat Generation. Mack was the quintessential New Yorker: street smart and at home anywhere, he cared little about what people thought of him and held an opinion on every subject. He was thought to be weird and was often openly characterized that way by conservative members of the student body. Yet it seemed that what he was called was the least important thing to him. These guys were so comfortable with themselves that one could easily find oneself emulating them and often did.

5

Oct. 12, 1965

Dear Folks,

Several things have happened since I last wrote you. We've just finished our Freshman class elections and I was elected Student Court Representative of the class. One person is elected from each of the four classes and are given the title "Court Representative" or "Justice."

We hold court, hear trials, and prosecute or pardon, just as a regular court. I didn't run for President of the Freshman class because the fellow who was running (and who won) was a person I felt would do a better job. (I have my doubts now, however). Other offices included Vice Pres, Sec'y, Asst. Sec'y, Treas, Bus. Mgr., Student Council Rep.   None of the other offices interested me except Pres. and Student Court Rep The Vice-Pres. and the Secretary are good friends of mine (so are the other) but these guys were in my building (really it's called a Unit). So three of the 8 class officers are in Unit 5.

Last weekend (Oct. 9 - 10) Wilkie came to the campus en route to Ft. Gordon in Augusta,, Ga. I was quite surprised to see him, had no idea he was coming. At night when we went to bed he slept in my bed while I slept on the top of my dresser. I woke up with a slight backache but I didn't mind too much. I also received a letter from Loleta from Southern U. Nothing in the letter of interest.

We had a football game last Friday. We were slaughtered by Hampton Institute, but I can't remember the final score. I think 18 - 6).

Above Our Heads

Is my coat and the shirts on the way (and anything else, those pair of stay—press pants I left)?

Maybe you might be interested in knowing the names of the officers of my class.

Pres.   Walter Dancy of Akron, Ohio
Vice-Pres. Connie Parsons of Birmingham, Ala.
Sec'y   George Watson of New York, N.Y.
Treas.   I don't know him
Student Council Rep. Don Hense Missouri
Student Court Me
Bus. Mgr Ken Powell Charlotte, N. C.

I will give you a brief biographical sketch of them later when I know them better. That's all.

           Love,
           Spencer

During the early weeks of the academic year, class elections took place in which the student court representative was elected among other class officers. This person would represent the class each year thereafter until graduation. Once the representative or "justice" reached the senior year, he became the chief justice and the senior class would elect a man to represent it on the court. So while there were always two persons without experience serving on the court, one had known Morehouse for three years. It was an effort at assuring that fairness would be reached in all decisions.

The student court at Morehouse was the administration's demonstration of confidence in our ability to discipline ourselves. In a curious sort of way it worked, although justice was dispensed in an arbitrary way since no written code was present on which the court might base its holdings. A student who was accused of some misconduct would be charged by the person whose "rights" had been violated. Typically, the violation was cutting line in the dining room. The truly serious disciplinary matters, such as cheating on exams were handled directly by the academic dean's office. The court was only permitted to decide upon those matters that did not have serious implications.

Once charged, the offender would appear before the five-member court in the presence of his accuser, usually after lunch on Sunday, and "argue" his position. He and the accuser would be permitted to bring witnesses. Some defendants secured the assistance of others who might more ably present their cases. If the charge was not successfully defended, the guilty student was "fined" one or more meal tickets, depending on whether there were unique circumstances, such as intimidation, violence or repeated offenses.

It was the possibility of losing a meal that dramatically grabbed the attention of the student body and caused the court to be taken seriously. No student wanted to lose a meal ticket. It was not that the meals served were so great, but rather that they had been paid for by either the parent or the student who worked to finance his education. In either case, it was a blow to one's pocketbook to be found guilty by the court. The student would have to purchase a meal in a place other than the school's dining room, where only meal tickets were received for fare. As a result, line-cutting was rare and disturbances in the dining room were for the most part non-existent. It was interesting that this tribunal was generally perceived to be fair-minded and never was held in disdain by the student body.

Above Our Heads

When my mother's youngest brother, Wilkie Byoune came to visit, it was my first opportunity to witness how the Morehouse community closes ranks. Though he was my relative and only five years my senior, he was treated as an outsider. At the time of his visit, I had only been at Morehouse a little over a month but had befriended a number of upperclassmen. These guys tolerated him because he was related to me, but they did not befriend him because he was not a part of our brotherhood. They attempted to lose him during the weekend that he visited.

I was told about a party that was going on that Saturday. They told me not to bring him. I was caught: he came to see me and I wanted to hang out with them because I knew it would be a great time. Later that evening, with Wilkie on the way to join us, we were all gathered in some guy's living room in an apartment off-campus. As we were discussing this matter, they proposed a charade. They would claim that they were going to get beer and instead keep going to the party. After a while, I was to go and look for them, suggesting that they should have returned by now. I, then, was to join them at the party.

I guess they had a ball. I did not see them until the afternoon of the next day. My uncle and I had a good visit, though after that experience, I would only invite females for visits to the college. It was simply beyond my ability to integrate males unconnected to Morehouse into our life.

6

Oct. 18, 1965

Dear Folks,

My roommate recently underwent a nervous or emotional breakdown and as a result is no longer at Morehouse. It seems that one night last week (I think Wednesday, the day of our first Humanities I test) he obtained liquor and got drunk. He caused quite a commotion (I wasn't in the room at the time, that's why) which caused two faculty members to come to our room. When Nick called one of them a "black nigger" they thought he was crazy and therefore took him to the psychiatric ward of the college infirmary. It was later found out (within two days) that he did show signs of mental illness and was then placed in Grady hospital. When he becomes well he will go to Louisiana to live with his sister or Bethel, Alaska, his original home.

We don't know the actual causes of Nick's "cracking up" but we can attribute a great deal to the academic pressures the school is placing upon us. I personally think that his was a social case as well as academic. Many of the students didn't accept him and this acceptance meant a lot to him.

I now have a room to myself but will soon be assigned another roommate. How are Marvin and

Above Our Heads

Billy? I told a girl that I had two younger brothers and that's all she asks about when I see her. She has a younger brother also.

Recently I received a letter from Mavis asking me to come to Fisk for their Homecoming this Saturday. I figure I would need about twenty to twenty-five dollars (cover bus fare and eating expenses. She stated that she could get me a room free of charge if I came). If you can't send the money I understand but I would appreciate it if you let me know. I had wanted to let Mavis know one way or the other the outcome.
Robert Cross told me you were going to come to our Homecoming Nov. 5-6. Is it true? He said that his parents called and that they said they saw your names on the list. If you can come that would be wonderful.

I'm going to start studying for a French test now so I'm going to end now.

Love,
Spencer

The ostracism of Nick ended in a drunken row. I am not certain that my presence in our room would have diverted Nick's behavior that night. His actions found support in his buddies, other guys who had experienced rejection by dorm mates in their settings. Understandably, these outcasts turned away from us. Though we were roommates, I was not to be a part of Nick's circle of friends.

Morehouse challenged the understanding of what a "nerd" was. A great many of the guys who attended were bespectacled, slide rule-carrying bookworms. To say that these fellows were snubbed because they were eggheads would not have been completely accurate. Most Morehouse students were bookish and an overwhelming number were also superb athletes and popular among men and women. These were the types that in high school everyone envied: unapologetically smart and immensely popular. Yet, at Morehouse, one was forced to make choices. With so many guys who were first and second in their high school graduating class and captain of the football team, one quickly realized that both of these distinctions would all too soon come to an end. Because one did not choose Morehouse to further develop athletic prowess (with an eye towards a sports career), entry into the school was the beginning of the choice-making process.

In this environment, men who had successfully masked their nerdiness could now give vent to it. Without losing their sense of balance but retaining their well-roundedness, guys pursued their chosen disciplines with a new-found passion. The passion was fueled by, among other things, the admiration in which college women, especially those at Spelman, held men who appeared bright and socially adept. This was the key to overall acceptance at Morehouse. Those who failed at campus life did so because they were not easily able to synthesize the dual demands of the academy: meeting the intellectual expectations and overcoming the emotional challenge.

The emotional challenges came in at least two forms: gaining acceptance of one's peers at Morehouse and feeling confident about how one was perceived by female students at any of the colleges in the Atlanta University Center. While a student did not have to have a positive personal relationship with every student at

Morehouse to be considered a "regular" guy or acceptable, they had to be perceived by the majority of students as a good fellow. Nick's problem was that he had too few relationships with any students and this fact frustrated any conscious or unconscious efforts he may have engaged in to build a reputation as "one of the guys."

If the campuses of the Atlanta University Center acted as learning laboratories, then the places beyond those communities served as proving grounds. My friend, Mavis Blake, the only other person in my high school class to attend a Black college, invited me for a football weekend at Fisk. Going beyond the boundaries of the familiar was the opportunity to test how much we had grown. Stated another way, it was the time Morehouse students could demonstrate how much more knowledgeable they were in the ways of the world than their counterparts in other colleges. This was not something one set out to do. When a guy visited another college, it was always to have serious fun. But I know that at times we did mental comparisons, designed to assure us that Morehouse was indeed all we believed her to be. More importantly, we were her products, every bit worthy of her reputation.

During the Sixties, at Black college football games, the drink of choice was the rum-'n-coke made with Bacardi rum and Coca-Cola. Morehouse men would pride themselves on being able to drink more of it than any one else and still be able to walk out of the stadium under their own power.

During this particular weekend in Nashville, I witnessed how important this Morehouse student's self-assigned accolade was. One of the freshmen who was part of the bunch I traveled with

The Making of a Morehouse Man

that weekend ended up getting so drunk that he passed out behind the stands in full view of anyone going to the bathroom (which was ultimately everyone). Every Morehouse student who saw him lying on the ground knew that he was a schoolmate. But the upperclassmen did not acknowledge him in such a way that others would know that the fellow attended Morehouse. They walked by him, ignoring his condition and refusing to come to his rescue. As they got drunk themselves, but still "proper," they began to lead the chiding that had begun to be directed against him. After a while, we who were his traveling companions could not take any more. We picked him up from the ground and placed him in a nearby parked car. All the time, we who helped him suffered similar verbal abuse from these same taunting upperclassmen. When our buddy awoke, we lit into him with fury for the embarrassment he caused us, hoping that together we did not cause undue shame to befall those who expected so much from us back in Atlanta.

ABOVE OUR HEADS

7

Oct. 28, 1965

Dear Folks,

I had a great time at Nashville. Arrived at 9 PM CST leaving Atlanta at 4:30 PM EST (5 hours). I managed to get a ride by a group of, you'll never guess, ALPHAS. When I got in Nashville it was too late too contact Mavis so I slept at a place the guys I went down with stayed.

I saw Mavis Saturday (I left Atlanta on Friday). Went to the Fisk-Howard game with her. Howard won 6-0. That evening I went to the Tennessee-Florida A&M game. Tenn. State won 46-6. Both bands were good. FAMU had the best marching, naturally, but Tenn. had the most orchestral-type sound. At this game all the MOREHOUSE MEN went as a unit and cheered for Tenn. State.

I didn't get any sleep that weekend and it showed when I came back. Tuesday I had a test in Algebra and I was still not fully alert because I didn't have enough sleep Monday   trying to review. (What I should have done, I imagine, was to sleep directly after classes on Monday).

The fellows decided to leave Nashville at 12:00 CST (midnight). We got in Atlanta in plenty of time before classes (7::00 EST) but with no rest. At least I will not make this same mistake a second time. I see the results can be devastating.

Financially, I did OK. I spent approx. $16.00:
    $8.00 - cost of transportation
    2.75 - cost of both game tickets
    3.00 - food
    2.25 - miscellaneous (approx.)
$16.00 (approx.)

I now have $5.00. If I need anymore I'll let you know, however, I understand the agreement was that this would be a sacrifice and that I would go without money for a couple of weeks. (So, this was not really extra money, was it?)

I received a letter from Mr. Weaver yesterday. He wants me to write him every now and then. Even though I dislike writing I feel the need to do so anyway. This is all for now.

Love,
Spencer

P.S. How are Marv and Billy? It's getting so I even miss them. That must mean it's getting pretty bad. Not really! When is my coat and shirts coming? It's getting real cold here!

That weekend was a complete Black College football weekend. At this time Howard, Fisk, Tennessee State and Florida A & M Universities all, in their unique ways, enjoyed a prominence that eluded Morehouse. The most obvious distinction lay in the fact that these schools were universities with graduate and professional divisions. Morehouse was only a four-year undergraduate college. The other schools were larger and

Above Our Heads

more wealthy, either because they were federally supported or, as in the case of Fisk, their alumni married well and could afford to make sizeable annual contributions to the school. (It was a commonly held belief that one of the attractions for women to attend Fisk was the abundance of eligible male medical and dental students at nearby Meharry Medical School. Before that weekend I had believed that Fisk was a women's school, as I had never heard of any men who were enrolled there.)

While I had now been a student at Morehouse for two months, I had never seen any celebrities in attendance at any of our games in Atlanta. In Nashville I saw Dionne Warwick and her entourage as well as Jerry Butler, the Chicago-based R&B singer. They simply blended in naturally to this slice of Black life as, well they should. It seemed that there existed in Nashville, for at least that weekend, a *savoir-faire* that the Atlanta scene did not have. In contrast to them, we were like their country cousins.

The men and women who attended college in Nashville proudly wore their money on their backs. I had never before seen so many well-dressed people. I remember overhearing people comment about how so-and-so must have been in front of the mirror for hours getting every curl of hair just right. And then someone else said the same thing about the guy she was with. As I looked around the crowd, I noticed these well-groomed people were the rule rather than the exception.

This is where I first saw a football tailgate party. Only this time, the tailgate was the trunk of a gorgeous, white MG roadster fully stocked with all of the popular potables of the day, including the ever-present rum-n-coke. The owner, the center of attention wearing appropriately a Burberry trenchcoat, held a small but animated group of coeds in rapt attention. My freshman brothers and I looked at this and simply shook our heads slowly, confessing that we had just witnessed another level of college life we all secretly swore to emulate as soon as we were able.

The most impressive events of the entire weekend were the halftime shows at both games. This was the time when the marching bands of rival schools could save the face of a losing team by performing their special magic upon the crowd. I was entranced. During this period, Florida A & M and Tennessee State had the Number One and Number Two marching bands in the entire country. The problem was that no one could agree on who was Number One and who was Number Two. Each band was musically brilliant but what distinguished them from all of the other college bands was an electrifyingly fast marching step that seemed more like a high-speed shuffle than a march. The drum major raised and lowered his staff a number of times in rapid succession, signaling the moment when the bands would enter onto the field. The marching musicians did so in an amazingly quick-cadenced, intricate pattern accompanied by the complex rhythmic beats of drums and cymbals, assembling in the center of the field, dust swirled all around them, settling back to earth many seconds after they had stopped to begin playing their first selection. This was simply amazing to see and was soon imitated by other bands, both Black and white. The Fighting Tigers of Morehouse College had been performing this routine early on, but it was in Nashville where the curve was set.

Of course there was a personal downside to the weekend. A classmate and I drove up to Nashville with a couple of fellows who were members of the Morehouse chapter of Alpha Phi Alpha

Above Our Heads

Fraternity. It was a common practice during this time for fraternity men to engage in a none-too-subtle "rush" of promising freshman candidates for membership in their chapters. Many of us were the recipients of random acts of generosity from guys we had befriended in various campus venues. When a new student was invited to attend a fraternity function by one of its members, it was a sincere effort to provide him an opportunity to look at life within that brotherhood. So when Bobby invited me to go to Fisk for the weekend, I agreed to do so primarily as a way of in my mind narrowing the selection as to the one fraternity I would ultimately pledge.

The five-and-a-half-hour car ride to Fisk provided these two guys ample time to feed my buddy and me the Alpha propaganda. Before I began at Morehouse, I had pretty much decided to pledge the fraternity most Chicagoans dreamed of pledging: Kappa Alpha Psi. But these guys were good. By the time we got to Nashville, I was giving serious consideration to joining Alpha. These fellows were not only among the best students on the campus but they really knew how to throw a party.

When we finally got to Nashville, we were given the royal treatment; their fraternity brothers greeted us like long-lost friends since Bobby and his fraternity brother who had traveled with us introduced us as candidates for the next Sphinx class, the fraternity's pledge club. They introduced us to female students at Fisk and Tennessee State who made us feel as if we belonged.

Around five o'clock Saturday morning I headed to the address where Bobby had prearranged for all of us to stay. We had gotten separated during the night, but good directions led me to an off-campus student housing complex. When I knocked on the door, dog-tired after my first night of carousing in what for me was a new city, I was told by a familiar voice that I would have to wait a few minutes before I could be let inside.

After three hours of sleeping on the steps of the porch outside the door, Bobby finally invited me in after the woman he had been with was finally out of bed, dressed and ready to head back to campus. It was nothing personal, I was told. At this point, I reasoned that I would not allow the experience to continue to ruffle me. During the ensuing hours, the decision about which fraternity to pledge had been made. For the longest time after this experience, Alphas were anathema to me. Thankfully, in time we grow beyond the moment when such experiences occur and come to realize that a grudge does not have to last forever.

Above Our Heads

8

Nov. 15, 1965

Dear Folks,

 I just received the letter you wrote in pencil. You have probably received my letter too. I mailed it just before I picked your letter up at the post office. I'm sure that letter expresses how I feel. I guess I perceived the idea of your wanting to know my feelings and wrote beforehand.
 I did receive the coat and shirts. And I enjoyed every one of those cookies. Looking forward to another batch. I also got the five dollars Dad sent about a week ago.
 I hope Daddy lands the job or whatever the exam was for that he's taking on Nov. 20.
 Granny Byoune and Grandmother both wrote day behind each other. Of course I told you in my last letter. I just wrote to acknowledge you.

Love,
Spencer

 P.S. I got a C in French. I don't feel like writing home anymore.

My first recorded grades were dismal. Except for the "C" in French, I cannot now remember what they were. I successfully blocked them from my memory. The French grade was particularly tough to accept since I believed that I was becoming rather proficient in it. It helped considerably to

The Making of a Morehouse Man

toss them in the garbage. It was not that I was this brilliant high school student, accustomed to receiving "straight-A's" before this time. It is that Morehouse inculcated within you this sense that you were brilliant (or could be if you simply did what you were able to do) and that you should receive "straight-A's." So, when you didn't, you became terribly disappointed, even when there was no evidence in the student's academic record that would reasonably justify the expectation of receiving "all-A's."

Everyone was made crazy at midterm time, especially the Freshman. It was the practice of Morehouse to send parents the first recorded grades from coursework taken by freshmen in the half-way point or mid-term of the first semester. The school did not tell us until the examination period, when all were in peril. Advance notice may not have made much difference. It seemed that everyone in all four classes adopted the same methodology of preparation during exam week: cram, cram, cram.

Some of these students were astounding at what they were able to do in a short space of time. In order to stay up all night, Howard Jeter would place volumes of encyclopedia on his bed so that if he was tempted to lie down upon it, he would be too uncomfortable to easily fall asleep. There were many guys who were able to re-read whole textbooks in a night and ace the final exam the next day.

Cecil Vernon Mason was one of those photographic minds. He was a fun-loving fellow throughout the school year who became deadly serious during exam time. He had the capacity to consume the important information for an entire semester's worth of instruction in two or three nights, and then amaze his classmates by scoring near the top each time.

Above Our Heads

I believe that for all of us the prime motivator in this frantic finals frenzy was fear. The principal fear, of course, was failure. Naturally, some were afraid of flunking out. Others, who had never received a grade below "B+," were desperately protecting their egos as they hoped their record of success would continue. Still others, like myself, did not want to suffer the admonishment of demanding parents. But then there was another group to which I had had little exposure prior to this time. There were those who came from austere poverty the likes of which I had only read about. These fellows would wear the same pair of pants and shirt for an entire week, because their wardrobe was so limited. These same young men grew up in homes built directly on the ground and they lived on dirt floors. They were the sons of families who had never had anyone before them attend college. An entire family's dreams rested upon a son's hope for success, not so much to become a lawyer, banker or doctor, but to simply become a college graduate. Yet, these same families were confident in the belief that the college would prepare their son for any graduate or professional study that he should choose.

The Making of a Morehouse Man

9

December 6, 1965

Dear Folks,

I was quite happy to receive the twelve dollars the last time, Daddy. I have saved ten dollars to defer some of my train expenses. By the way had you planned to send me my train ticket, and/or request me to make reservations. Whatever you decide it would be good to think along the lines of a one-way ticket. If I had a round—trip ticket for the train I would have to catch the train back here on or before New Year's Day. I had thought of taking the plane back which would enable me to leave the day before I was due back in school. This would be possible since I'd be working the holiday season.

I have enclosed a letter which I had written about two weeks ago. [Note: this is the letter beginning Chapter Eight.] Disregard most of it, for you can see it's contradictory content. I just thought you'd like to know my feelings at that time.

I still haven't got all of my grades but I'm sure they're not bad.

Still no girl friends. My mood changes from day to day too much to have a girl who could understand me. I'm not choicy it's just that I feel a boy-girl relationship is a two-way street. She would be giving of herself all of the time but I wouldn't always have such steady responses.

This is the entire relationship and without it there is nothing. Therefore, until I get situated (academically as well as social) I won't be looking for a perpetual friendship with "une femme."

Above Our Heads

    I'm not good a(t) writing character sketches, especially of these fellows at M'house, so I will tell you all about them at Christmas. Tell Mr. Weaver I haven't forgotten about him and that I want very much to write him but you know I hate writing letters anyway. There are several things I want to discuss with him concerning the campus fads and congratulate (sic) him on the predictions he had given me earlier but that I didn't heed them. The circular wire-rimmed glasses, striped pants, shorter suit jackets, etc. I will try to write him a letter before I come home.
    How are Marvin and Billy getting along? I know they are doing well in school but how are their characters developing? Are they asking more and more questions? Getting any answers? I may write before I come home to confirm plans for coming home.

                                            Love,
                                            Spencer

During my high school years, I had the good fortune of meeting a number of older gentlemen, most of whom were my parents' friends or friends of the family. One such person was Mr. Reginald Weaver, a teacher who had worked with my mother who was at the time the principal at James Whitcomb Riley Elementary School in Markham, Illinois. Mr. Weaver was the perfect primary schoolteacher: he was young, loved children, knew all of the latest fads and simply enjoyed people and his work. For a long time after I was an adult, I would continue to call this man, now my contemporary, Mr. Weaver. His contribution to my life was important in readying me for the social swim at Morehouse. He taught me how to buy good clothing without regard for the "name-brand," but rather with an understanding of materials, quality of workmanship and style. He impressed upon me the value of being down-to-earth and the pitfalls of trying to impress people with how smart you thought you were. Mr. Weaver loved music and knew all the artists, what tunes were hot and all the latest dance steps. He loved to party and took me on many occasions to his hometown of Danville, Illinois, where I was privileged to meet his family. His was a warmth I was privileged to experience at a critical stage in my development. To this day, he is an extremely accomplished leader in public education, which I believe is the result, not just of his industry, but of his knowledge of people and his ability to give them what they need even though they may at first not want it. Mr. Weaver helped me to make the transition from home to college with the "education" he provided beyond the classroom and my home.

Toward the end of the first semester of study, my classmates and I began to feel that we had gone through something quite dramatic. Now, I would refer to it as a life-changing experience. Then, I would simply have to term it growing older - not simply in a chronological sense (indeed, at that age one was young forever), but in an emotional sense that I could not yet explain. Within a very short space of time we were examining all of the life issues. Without prodding from our parents, we were doing what all parents hope their children do sooner than later: take a serious look into our future.

We had all gone through the first round of testing. Once the facts were revealed, we soon learned the truth behind the myth. Some of us were more scholarly than others. While all of us had

Above Our Heads

been accepted to this mythical place on the belief that we were the best, in a very real way, there was soon to be discovered by all of us that a pecking order existed in the rarefied air of the Morehouse freshman class.

Of course, on a purely intellectual level, we all realized that there could only be one "Number One." Yet it was our hope, and no one really thought too long about this, that it would occur like a roll of the dice: somehow all of us would shine brightest at one time or another. Each of our turns would come in time. Ultimately, however, we understood that some would have to settle for second best.

The fact of the matter was that many of those who were in the Class of '69, while good students, had quite a bit to learn about being great students. And some of us never would be. Yet this was our first semester and no one, thankfully, was to dwell upon this reality until much later.

At this time the airline industry was beginning to mount an intense campaign to woo train travelers away from the rails and into the air. With the "youth fare" promotions of the major airlines, it was becoming cheaper to fly round-trip rather than to take the train. I loved train travel, but I also wanted to get back and forth quickly and save precious dollars. A fear of flying was virtually non-existent.

By the end of the first semester, we were all ready to get boarding passes out of Atlanta to all points. We were actually looking forward to returning to the oft-forgotten familiarity of three mandatory meals and minor rivalries from siblings. I was returning to Chicago to the best time of the year to be in Chicago: the Christmas season. And to make it that much better, I was returning as a Morehouse man.

10

Jan. 10, 1966

Morehouse College
Atlanta, Georgia 30314

Dear Folks,

    This is my first real opportunity to write. I fell right into my old routine upon returning to Morehouse - study late, sleep little. It is now 4:45 AM Monday morning Jan. 10. I've just completed another term paper and my French lesson. I was getting ready to study a bit of British literature (The Tempest, Shakespeare). I'm taking a break to write this short letter while listening to "Song of My Father" by Horace Silver on my roommate's, Steve's, new record player.

    It's very quiet except for the record and a rustling of leaves as the wind blows them along the walks. It is the only peaceful time when one can reflect on the day's activities and lose sleep in the process. My Sunday was pretty filled. I attended a meeting of the Student Court which really never started because the person to be tried did not show. He will be sapiened (wrong spelling).

    I balanced that grade in math I told you about with a 100% on the second test. I just have to get a 100% on the semester test to get an "A" in math. Oh BROTHER!!! Dr. Hume and her English class is giving me the roughest time here.

    I am contemplating transference. I just can't afford to have a "C" in English next semester. Maybe I just look at it with such a pessimistic attitude that I won't

Above Our Heads

do any better. I don't know. But she is really pouring it on now.

How do you like the stationery? Some sheets are without a crest in the corner like this one, but it is of good quality paper.

This is the first letter that I have written to anyone so don't feel slighted (not that I'm so much). I'll try to write Granddaddy and Grandmother and the others some time but I usually don't have the time. When I take time to write at all it's usually for a professor. I feel pretty bad about not seeing or writing Mr. Weaver. He may receive a letter the same time you get this one.

Send my Bedspread and Sterno Stove. My roommate and I are making an attempt at creating a plush room in which to attack our struggle with education. I don't know where the Sterno stove is but I believe that it may be in my knapsack under the workbench in the basement.

It's now 5:15. I know that it hasn't taken but about 2 or 3 minutes to read up to this point if
that long, but I found it difficult to find anything to write about when there is virtually nothing.
Anyway I'm getting sleepy.

How is everything at home? Who's winning the most argument, Marvin, between Mom and Dad? I won't even ask how Marv and Billy are doing in school. I know that it's above average work. Encourage, them, however to read on a higher level then they are at (Thoreau for instance or Hemingway).

It will get them in the right frame for handling the really great thinkers like George Santayana and John Dunn. Insist that they read and write about what they read FOR YOU TO HELP THEM. It will be invaluable to them. Stress too that they should mix social (parties, movies, etc.) with that just as much. NOTH-

The Making of a Morehouse Man

ING IN EXCESS.
    I'm no great teacher so I'll stop now. By the way how is the great teacher. At U. of C. yet giving the profs a hard time? Did you get that Postal Service Officer job, Dad? I'm sure the noble citizens of Markham envy the both of you.
    I don't feel like working for Mr. Marks anymore at this point. I recently had a bad dream that I was working for him at a drug store, no less, sweeping floors. I just couldn't stand it this next summer. Not now anyway. Take care.

Your Son,
Spencer

While being at home for the Christmas holiday season was a welcomed change of pace from studies, it was great to be back in Atlanta. Even in January it was mild enough on some days to go about in shirt sleeves; a stark contrast to the crushing cold of Chicago during that month. I was now beginning to equate Atlanta with home. It did not fully replace my parents' home nor could it have. But this was the point: their home was theirs. And Morehouse was not, nor ever could become, my parents' home, it was mine. I had recently begun to understand the house where I lived with my parents and brothers as the home belonging to my mother and father. At Morehouse, where I would live three-fourths of the year, I felt that I had discovered home - my physical, emotional and spiritual base from which the rest of my life would emerge.
    The second semester began with a new roommate. Stephen

Above Our Heads

Johnson grew up in Queens, New York in a section called Jamaica. His father was a prominent minister of the United Church of Christ and pastored a rather significant congregation. Steve carried himself in the manner of one who came from a privileged setting. He had excellent taste in clothing and had an impressive wardrobe that proved it. He was a cross-country runner and quite a good one, having come to Morehouse from an award-winning high school track team of which he was captain. Tall and good-looking, he was never at a loss for female companions. This guy was the quintessential man's man. Other guys either envied or admired him and women swooned.

When Nick's departure left me without a roommate, the housing officer gave me the option of inviting a classmate of my own choice. I had not really become friends with Steve during the first semester but we connected on this clothes thing. He was a traditional dresser: wool, cotton, silk from the venerated stores such as Brooks Brothers, Abercrombie & Fitch, etc. At that time I had never heard of some of the stores from where he purchased his clothes: J. Press, Paul Stuart, Aquascutum, those exclusively New York City shops. A Chicagoan, I knew of the national stores but was fascinated to learn that there were stores that could mount a challenge to Brooks Brothers. So we roomed together. I figured that I could always learn more. Why not, then, from someone who wore the natural shoulder look, well, naturally?

Steve's steady girlfriend was an absolutely gorgeous woman. They seemed perfectly matched. She was a tall, willowy freshman from Spelman with old money breeding. When they were on the dance floor together, magic happened. It was as though they had done nothing for a week but practice the way they would look when they danced together. At moments like those, everyone wanted to be them.

Not too long into the semester, our relationship began to show signs of wear. Even though I had grown up in what was then the second largest city in the U.S., I was just not quick enough for Steve. He was a big man on campus even as a freshman because of his emerging reputation as a track star. In comparison, I was a nobody. I guess I had become quite a bore to Steve. Soon we found that not even our appreciation for the same kind of clothes was enough to fuel what we had believed began as a friendship. After that semester we would not room together and would cross paths infrequently over the next three years.

My circle of friends was beginning to become comprised of those who pursued literary interests. I still continued to be a part of the Canterbury House crowd, even when other influences daily challenged that association. I don't believe that Steve ever set foot inside the Canterbury House. If Morehouse was a place wherein there was an acceptance of "nerd-types," Canterbury House was ecstatic over our presence.

11

Jan. 24, 1966

Dear Folks,

    Thank you very much for the money, Dad. I've opened a savings account at a local bank [Citizens Trust Company] for all the money I don't spend. In this way you will not need to send any extra money.
    Sorry I forgot to tell you about my arrival to Atlanta. You may not believe it but I spent twenty-four hours (24) on that train. The train took the wrong track and bypassed Chattanooga by about 75 to 100 miles. Naturally we had to backup in order to let the people off in Chattanooga. It wasn't really too bad, however, I did meet several nice girls and there were a great deal of other people who were very friendly (I imagine so being together twenty—four hours).
    I tried to hold off writing until I was sure of my grades. Yesterday I was quite optimistic; today after registering for my new courses it's a different story. I was hoping for Dean's List (but I'm really not sure but with my luck, Oh, well):

HRS.			
3	162	Algebra II	C
3	152	French	B
3	161	Humanities I	B
3	161	Social Science	B
3	153	Eng. Comp.	? (most likely-C)
2	153	Health Education	B
		(maybe A, speculative)	
1	151	Phys. Ed.	B
18			

This semester I'm taking fifteen hours. I desired to take nineteen but there were no courses I could take (the courses offered were either on the junior level or above. The sophomore courses were only offered if you had the first semester of the course and during the second semester only the second semester was offered in a course. Those that offered the first semester of the course now I had required courses which conflicted with them.). Also, Dr. Kennedy, my best friend on the faculty advised me that I should rest this semester (can you believe that; I can't even see how I am working that hard. My grades certainly don't reflect it).

The Dean's List must not want me on it. There should be no excuse, however this next semester (and even if I do make it I won't get a scholarship. You have to be on it two consecutive semesters.

Here's my new schedule:

	9:40	10:40	11:40	1:45	2:45	3:45
Mon	Eng		Soc		French	Sci
Tues	Trig		Soc	Hum. I		Sci Lecture
Wed	Eng		Soc		French	Sci
Thur	Trig		French	Hum.I Lecture		
Fri	Eng		French			
Sat	Trig			Hum. Lecture		

The title of those courses:

Trigonometry (Trig) is called Transcendental Functions.

English Composition (I'm keeping the same teacher with the idea that I won't let her whip me).

Social Science under Dr. Melvin Kennedy (He was my teacher the 1st semester also).

ABOVE OUR HEADS

Humanities I.
French II (I'm taking the 1st semester of second year French. Plan to go to Thornton or some other college at home and take the second semester to finish my language requirement.

Once again I passed the reading test (three hours which I am exempt from taking the Remedial Reading class).

All of these classes are three-hour courses. So you can see where the fifteen come. I could not take physical education this semester (offered at 2:45 on Monday because of my French class which meets at 3:45 the same day. You see P.E. lasts until 4:30 and Dr. Kennedy suggested that three hours of French are more important than one hour credit in Phys. Educ.

I'm really doubtful as to whether or not I want to stay here four years. The way these few courses are arranged I'd be five years getting out of here. However, I'd love to have a Morehouse degree. They're becoming more and more impressive and important.

If I have any problems I'll let you know.

You know Mother I had the most terrible dream about you. The fellows in my dorm were all standing out in front of our building where we were being spoken to by President Mays. All of a sudden someone ran out of the dormitory shouting that I had a phone call. When I asked to be excused Pres. Mays wouldn't let me go. I went anyway feeling that it was something important. When I reached the phone it was you Mom. You said what I now believe is the most frightening thing I ever heard. You said,"Now don't laugh when I tell you but the doctor said that I only have one more month to live." These words frightened me so much I woke up crying (and ran to the phone trying to call you to tell you I wasn't laughing in my sleep). There is no phone in my dorm. This happened about a week ago but I knew you would just laugh and think it quite ridiculous when I told you. Anyway I hope you are doing fine and are not ill. I remember wanting to quit school because Mays would not let me answer the phone in that dream.

I've used practically all of my paper but I got a great deal off my mind.

I'm really glad to hear of your success, Dad. I'm sure that you will be happy at whatever job you take. I'm sending the W-2 form back to you. I can't find time to get 1040 and of course you know I would appreciate it if you took care of that matter. I understand that I must sign the completed form and send it to the government.

I hope that Marv is better and Bill is doing fine. Tell Pepper to stay healthy.

Love,
Spencer

P.S. Did I omit anything?

The worst thing that I could have done in registering for the second semester was to limit myself to fifteen hours. I should have figured out a way of getting another class on my schedule. Though I was running scared the entire first semester, it was that fear that compelled me to work. Yet there was a perfectly good reason why I registered for the minimum full-time load: Springtime and Spelman.

The upperclassmen who befriended freshmen were enormously helpful in assisting your trek through the first year. In fact, what they did was teach you everything that you needed to know to negotiate the remaining years and have fun in the process. One of the lessons was to register in the Fall semester for as many hours as you could stand to work without becoming brain dead. Though the Fall and Winter climates in Atlanta were not harsh, the first semester was understood as an "indoor" period, except for the football games. For the most part, one was geared to being inside and therefore more likely than not to be predisposed to studying. Therefore, (the reasoning went), if you are going to be "forced" by temperatures to be inside more than outside, then take a greater load and use the confinement for study. Somehow, this seemed to make sense. In this way, too, if you had to repeat a course, you could do so in the following semester and still possibly maintain the thirty hours of course credit per year necessary for graduating within the hoped-for four-year timetable. If you did not have to repeat a course, you were clearly ahead of the game with reserve credits.

Following this logic, a student was greatly rewarded if he passed all of his courses in that first semester. Not only would he have made significant progress toward graduating, but he could now register for the minimum number of 15 hours (to hold full-time status) in the Spring semester. This was vitally important for most of us. For even though the Spring semester contained the Winter season, it contained the warmest months of the academic year. When Spring had sprung, students moved outside and Spelman women began to shed their winter garments in favor of more flattering attire. So it was in the Morehouse student's best interest to take fewer courses in the second semester so as not to miss the incredible climate that awaited, both weatherwise and socially.

Taking 18 or more hours per semester at Morehouse was not the easiest task in the world to accomplish. I felt particularly relieved when my social science professor, Dr. Melvin Kennedy, who had befriended me toward the end of my first semester, advised me that I had worked pretty hard during my first year of college. He indicated that I could take a break by registering for 15 hours. After all, I was still undergoing an adjustment process from life at home. He was so right. I was studying hard, but that was not what made college so draining. I was also questioning on a daily basis what it all meant, and it was this that wore me out, along with my classmates.

The content of the coursework was not as difficult as juggling it with one's growing relationship to the larger context of the college community. Formal classroom instruction, while undeniably and obviously essential to the collegiate experience, found itself in competition with the psycho-physiological development of 900 young men.

Thinking about women seemed to occupy most of our waking hours. The way we dressed was calculated to impress women. The way we spoke, behaved, the interests we sought, were seemingly all done to capture the attention of our counterparts at Spelman. It was not as though we did not regard the women in the other schools of the Atlanta University Center as eligible. Primarily, there were two reasons for why we focused on Spelman women: tradition and the men in the other schools.

Above Our Heads

It was thought to be a given that the Morehouse man would date a Spelman woman. These were the liaisons that led to marriage, families and future generations of Morehouse and Spelman students. But equally important was the presence at Morris Brown and Clark of male students who frowned upon Morehouse fellows dating women in their schools. Spelman students let it be known that they were less interested in guys from schools other than Morehouse. Yet, ironically, women in the coed schools quietly preferred to date Morehouse men. These facts combined to create a resentment by male students in the other schools toward Morehouse. So, in a way, we were limited to Spelman (but I never ever heard anyone complain about it).

Yet, we were frustrated. We not only found ourselves in competition with our upperclass brothers at Morehouse for Spelman love, but we soon discovered that we competed among ourselves, more often than not, for the same person. We were frustrated.

12

Feb. 16, 1966

Dear Folks,

I believe I made the Dean's List! The grades will be mailed home soon.

I desire to pledge Kappa Alpha Psi. I am going to at least write my letter to the fraternity [which states why you want to be a Kappa] and go for my interview. All I said was that I desire to pledge. I want your okay or advice as to why I should or shouldn't. felt that while I had this "B" average that pledging now would not affect my overall average for the Freshman year.

Then too, I may not get another "B" average very soon as the coursework becomes increasingly difficult. Also, Bill Baldon and Reginald should be coming home as Kappa's and even though I wouldn't be "made" I would still be a Scroller.

Please write soon as the line will be forming for the Spring pledgees for Kappa Alpha Psi.

There is a fellow here at Morehouse named Curtis Martin. He's from Chicago. His parents are Vivian and Marion Martin. His father is an electrician. Do you know them? I just met him a few weeks ago. Pretty nice fellow.

Please do not send any more checks...only money orders. Even though I have an account at a local bank [Citizens Trust Company] I have to wait six days for the check to be cleared as it is from an out-of-town bank account. Would appreciate gratefully.

Possess an uncontrollable dislike for Dr. [Miss] Hume, my English teacher. Realize it's not healthy and am trying to overcome it. Find it difficult.

Above Our Heads

What happened to the package you were supposed to send? You were just kidding me is that it?
How is everyone?
Still no girl friend, however, a couple are out there trying. First had to see how I could make it through a semester. I'm partially satisfied. Will try to improve.

Love
Spencer

P.S. I heard from Dad. He's been traveling a great deal. Seemed to have a good time. Sent a beautiful post card.

During this time, and I believe even now, Chicago's Black college fraternity of choice was Kappa Alpha Psi. The historic reason for this was the simple fact that it was founded at Indiana University in 1911. Two years later, the second chapter was established at the University of Illinois. As a result, there was every opportunity for African-American students who attended these schools in large numbers over a period of many years to establish the prominence of Kappa throughout the region, which included its largest city, Chicago. The other major Black college fraternities, though prevalent by the Sixties throughout the nation, had begun in Eastern universities and largely because of this, did not have the historical reinforcement enjoyed by Kappa Alpha Psi in the Midwest.

Everyone I knew growing up in Chicago either wanted to be a Kappa or pledged Kappa. To pledge a fraternity was not simply to promise to be a faithful member; it was to undergo a period of time wherein one was given the opportunity to demonstrate a

The Making of a Morehouse Man

commitment through word and deed. It would be an absolute violation of an obsessively guarded secret for me to reveal what one must demonstrate to fulfil the pledge, except to reiterate that which was public knowledge. Yet, needless to say, a chapter of a fraternity founded at an all-male school would be among the most rigorous of physical, mental and emotional trials for a college student to undergo. And it was.

The pledge class of Kappa Alpha Psi was called the Scrollers Club. It existed in the same manner from chapter to chapter. It possessed its own traditions, songs, handshake, secrets, insignia - all of the things necessary to bring people together into a community. It was not called male-bonding then, but that's exactly what it was. We loved it.

At Morehouse, in the school year 1965-1966, there were chapters of all four of the major college Greek-letter fraternal organizations founded by Black students for purely social and civic purposes. Omega Psi Phi, Alpha Phi Alpha and Phi Beta Sigma were present and each, like Kappa, had its unique traditions and pledge clubs through which men gained entrance into their private circles. The competition for recruiting members from the ranks of the freshmen class was not very aggressive. At other schools, particularly white colleges and universities, the recruitment of new members to fraternities and sororities was called the "rush." Students at Morehouse seemed to instinctively know to which fraternity they belonged. It was not especially a "good" or a "bad" thing to pledge to one fraternity over another. All were so different that it was more like finding and associating with one's sense of corporate identity. As the national myth went, and perhaps still persists, the Alphas were the bookworms, the Omegas were the wildest partyers, the Kappas had the unfortunate reputation of being drunkards and the Sigmas were rather a nondescript bunch of what might be accurately identified as simply "nice guys."

The members of Kappa Alpha Psi at Morehouse comprised the Pi Chapter. This was the first chapter of the fraternity to be established in a Southern college. I had decided before I had left Chicago that I would pledge Kappa. It was reassuring to know that nothing I had witnessed about the men of Pi challenged my goal. Indeed, I looked upon these guys as the most incredible fellows of the upper classes. While the other fraternities seemed to be easily pigeon-holed as to the types that they attracted, Kappas seemed to be of all types. Among them were some of the best athletes, brightest students and most popular men on the campus. After I had become a Kappa and had become acquainted with persons from the other fraternities, I realized that they, too, had their fair share of these types as well. Yet what continued to remain the most important distinction for Kappa was the fact that among its membership could be found the most original thinkers at Morehouse.

In three of my four years the student body president was a Kappa. Throughout my years at Morehouse, members of my fraternity held high profile leadership positions. I had represented my class on the student court, becoming chief justice in my senior year. It seemed typical for a Kappa to recite poetry, sing in the glee club, play football, party all night and get up the next morning and set the curve on the calculus final. While now it seems ludicrous to think that because a man would be interested in the arts he should not find stimulation on the gridiron, in 1965, this was an eye-opener for me. It seemed as though life prior to this time was all so parochial, so restricted in the way it was viewed and lived.

While the other fraternities seemed to capitalize upon their reputations, using them as a means for providing themselves with a corporate profile, and hence, securing their unique identities, Kappas at Morehouse appeared to challenge at every opportunity the public's perception of themselves. This was evidenced by the fact that the chapter admitted, from among those qualified to pledge, every category of student who then existed. There were the athletic types like Charles Cabbage and Juan Lieba; the scholars, too numerous to mention, but which certainly included guys like Jimmie Millhouse, Nelson Taylor, James Gray, and Sanford Bishop; and there was simply every other kind of person from the radical activist to the politically conservative, the wallflower to the "life-of-the-party," and a range of folks in between. Yet, as I have suggested, each of these guys, more often than not, was a composite of all of these elements in greater or lesser measure. Interestingly enough, the brothers of Pi seemed to blend together to create a harmonious whole.

Dr. Jeanette Hume, my first year English professor and a graduate of Randolph-Macon Women's College, was among my most demanding teachers in the first year. Though I believed that she contributed most to my growing appreciation for the written word, I began to loathe her. During the second semester, I believed that I was doing some of my best work in her class but it was never good enough to satisfy her. Nevertheless, I did not have a leg to stand on to support my dislike for her. After all she came highly recommended: a Masters and Ph.D. from Yale. More importantly, my classmates were simply better students and they

Above Our Heads

regarded her highly.

Ours was a writing class, English Composition. I could not believe how extraordinarily able these guys were at putting together well-crafted essays. It was this experience, as much as any other, that successfully challenged my firmly-held, northern-bred bias that precluded the possibility that articulate proponents of written English could come from the deep South, notwithstanding Hurston and Faulkner. I remember one instance in which we were required to write an introspective piece regarding some part of our lives. Perhaps I did not understand what was being asked of us, but I wrote two-and-a-half pages on my view of the Vietnam War and its direct effect upon me. It was mediocre, if not whiny, and gained me the expected "C." One of my classmates wrote 10 pages on everything that he was thinking and feeling within a five minute period. He wrote in great detail about the sounds outside and the smells he was experiencing in that moment and how these sensations caused him to recall other events. His exceptionally probing essay earned him an "A" and was for a long time thereafter applauded by our professor as a model essay of this kind of "stream of consciousness" writing.

13

Morehouse College
Atlanta, Georgia

Feb. 28, 1966

Dear Folks,

    I will begin the pledge period today (5 weeks). I will not become a member of Kappa, however, until September when I return (the policy for Freshman). This means that I will not have to pay anything but ten (10) dollars for pledge fees. The remaining ninety dollars will be paid when I become a Kappa. I will work for that this summer. I have already paid my ten dollars.
    I hesitated to tell you before but I was working at the library for two months (received a total income of 33 dollars during that time; wage $.50/hr). I didn't want to tell you because if my grades had been poor you would have probably attributed it to the job. If I had desired to pledge you could have easily thrown that up in my face as a preventative for such an action (as pledging).
    With that money (the 33 dollars) I was able to buy a few books for the new semester as well as pay my pledge fees. I quit the job so too much of my time would not be occupied.
    Find out from George where his relatives live (the exact address, please). Also, ask him about that job he was talking to me about where he works. I want to get several things this summer and I'll need more money than what Marks pays.
    Ask Mrs. Baldon and Mrs. Mitchell where Billy and

Above Our Heads

Reginald live. Several times I could (or needed to) write them.

Granny Byoune wrote me and said that she sent five dollars to you. Yet, you only purchased two pair of two dollar socks. I understand if you needed the extra dollar but I wish you would have told me.

Do you enjoy the new job, Dad? I'm still holding you to your promise about giving me your pin (Kappa) but there are surely a great deal of fancy pins that are not all tarnished like yours. Anyway, yours has W. Gibbs inscribed on the back. I want one with S. Gibbs.

How are Marv and Bill? Is Marv reading more. And I don't mean anything from MY BOOK HOUSE. Introduce him to some "hard" books and discuss them with him (e.g. The Man, Armageddon, Herzog, really I mean it). He has a great deal of time that I'm sure is being wasted. Also start him to read things about the Black man's plight. (Eg. A Rage in Harlem by Chester Himes, The Black Anglo-Saxons by Nathan Hare and also the older books in your own library.

How's Granddaddy and Grandmother? I realize I haven't written them but like you they believe I should write before they will write. (that's a poor philosophy).

Love,
Spencer

It was the job at Trevor Arnett Library that began my unceasing love for libraries. I had used libraries as an elementary school student, favoring their quiet solemnity instead of the after-school chaos of kids. There was the old Carnegie Public Library in Harvey, Illinois with well-worn, heavy leather-upholstered chairs in which I loved to doze off while trying to study.

The Making of a Morehouse Man

This place remained my friend until my senior year in high school. Yet, when I got that work-study student job at Trevor Arnett Library, my delight in libraries began to soar.

I found that I actually enjoyed wheeling the heavily-burdened library cart filled with oversized reference books that needed to be reshelved in the stacks. They represented sources of information I never knew existed. The stacks in themselves were simply fascinating. Into these one would enter and immediately the outside world would be completely shut out. It was a place with all types of cubbyholes for curling up in to study and booklined passageways into which one could become totally lost to all but the project that occasioned the visit. Here was the place in which I spent some of my most satisfying and meditative moments.

The Trevor Arnett Library was a facility owned by Atlanta University but was built on land immediately adjacent to Morehouse. While it was intended for use by the entire Atlanta University student population, it appeared to be an extension of the Morehouse campus because of its close proximity to it. While Morehouse had a library-type facility known as the Reading Room, it was an unadorned, austere place where none but the seriously studious would venture to go. Trevor Arnett, save the stacks, was like a great social hall. When gathered here on the pretext that one was preparing for class, people met, gossiped, planned parties, courted and, on rare instances, made love.

This was the Sixties! The banner cry throughout most American colleges was "Make Love, not War!" Many of us took this message to heart. While fellows confided in me that they had taken a woman to a deserted floor in the stacks for sex, this was not the most exotic library locale for this event to take place.

Above Our Heads

Trevor Arnett was blessed to have a beautifully designed and landscaped plaza setting off its entrance. Many of the Canterbury crowd, among others, would while away a hot Saturday afternoon spread upon a blanket picnic-style drinking beer in this garden-like setting. The foliage of bushes and trees was lush and plentiful and repeated itself completely around the four sides of the building. It provided the perfect cover for having an intimate liaison under the stars, completely undetectable by others. Indeed, learning took a variety of forms at Trevor Arnett Library.

My already well-established ego was growing by leaps and bounds. It is incredible what a couple of good grades can do for one's attitude. How I believed that I could tell my parents how to educate my brothers is to my mind now, quite frankly, obnoxious. Yet, life within the classroom and life outside it were beginning to feed upon one another. I was applying my formal instruction to conversations that I was having among people in a variety of informal settings. I was beginning to believe that I could make contributions to the way people thought about things and even to the way they went about their daily activities.

The Making of a Morehouse Man

14

Morehouse College
Atlanta, Georgia

Mar. 8, 1966

Dear Folks,

I hope you can understand that pledging is taking up a great deal of my time. All my letter-writing time, therefore, is merged with the time I give as a Scroller (the Kappa pledgee).

There are thirteen fellows pledging on the Kappa line. This is the longest line in the history of Pi chapter (Morehouse College chapter of K A Psi). The names and other information about them are as follows:

1) Tommie Pye - Freshman - Atlanta, Ga.
2) Milton Wilkins - Freshman - St. Louis, Mo.
3) Mark Hill - Junior - Birmingham, Ala.
4) Arthur O'Keefe - Freshman - Boston, Mass. Incidentally, the only white boy in the Freshman class)
5) Sanford Bishop - Sophomore - Mobile, Ala.
6) Jimmie Milhouse - Sophomore - Columbia, S.C.
7) Richard Hudlin - Sophomore - St. Louis, Mo.
8) Billy Charles Gilbert - Freshman - Monroe, La.
9) James Hawes III - Freshman - Elberton, Ga.
10) Me
11) Isaac Joe - Sophomore - Bishopville, S.C.
12) Delano Raines - Junior - Savannah, Ga.
13) Thomas M. Watson — Sophomore - Athens, Ga.
This is according to height, smallest to tallest.

Above Our Heads

I only have to worry about two of the big brothers causing me any physical harm. But this year they are supposed to stop brutality. So far none has occurred.

I'm sure my average will suffer but I believe I can average at least a 2.5 (C+) for the entire year. What they plan to do is let us participate in everything but the actual initiation. This will occur next year when will then be formally Kappa's. This will apply only to Freshmen. Ordinarily the school's policy is to belay the freshmen in participating in the Hell Week exercises and wait until the first semester of their sophomore year to go through all of that. By doing it like that we will avoid spending more time away from our studies and at the same time be recognized as Kappas at Morehouse by Pi Chapter.

I cannot reveal some of the things they have made us do in pledge club meetings but a usual day consists of:

a) 6:00 Awake
b) 6:10 - 6:30 Awake all Big Brothers for breakfast
c) 6:30 - 7:30 Breakfast
d) 7:30 - 4:00 Classes, review or study, nap and eat lunch
e) 4:00 - 5:30 Free (unless Big Brothers don't have you running an errand for them)
f) 5:30 - 6:30 Eat dinner
g) 7:00 - 10:00 Study in Library
h) 10:00 - 12:00 Run errands at snack shops for Big Brothers. On Monday at this time pledge club meeting.

Everyone will probably make it but each day gets rougher and rougher. Enclosed you will find some material concerning a Civil Service Test that I took and passed. Instead of writing a lot of mess I decided to let you see it, comment, and send it back. While reading the instructions realize that I desire to work in Berkeley, Calif. since Aunt Grace lives there and she has offered me several invitations. It is not necessary to fill out anything, however, look for a place for signature. I am at the library right now and don't have the forms with me so I can't say whether such a blank space exists or not. Will right again as soon as the opportunity presents itself.

Love,
Spencer

P.S. Any word on Tax Returns.

Pledging was a blast! The fraternity experience was the great leveling event at Morehouse. This was the opportunity wherein all facets of college life were brought together in one organizational structure. Here existed the athletes, the scholars, the musicians, the people with whom one's own limiting dormitory existence would prevent you from naturally interacting. In the first year at Morehouse social life revolved around the events that you and your dormmates created. As you became acclimated to the larger environment, you might find yourself at parties that would take you beyond your sheltered core. Yet these occasional exposures could rarely sustain relationships with upperclassmen. Association with these fellows, however, increased one's popularity throughout the college community. This then was the importance of pledging the fraternity as soon as possible.

At Morehouse a freshman could pledge in the second semester, but only if he had at least a 3.0 G.P.A. or "B" average earned in the first semester. The theory was that if, in the second semes-

Above Our Heads

ter, the pledgee received a "D" average, he would still end the year with a "C" and thus return to the college without probationary status. We were so anxious to become members of a pledge class, that we failed to see the lunacy of this reasoning. Every Freshman everywhere needs to devote as much time to classwork as possible without mindless distractions during the crucial first year of college.

There was a great deal of time spent in what seemed at first like time-wasters. Often, usually at the initial days of the pledge period, a pledgee might be requested by a Big Brother (a member of the fraternity) to count the number of bricks in the wall of a building. Pledgees actually would stand in front of a building and count the bricks. This was, of course, highly amusing to the one who made the request and anyone who chanced to witness it.

"Scroller, count the bricks in the front wall of Robert Hall."

"Yes, Big Brother. One, two, three... (and 30 minutes later)...585, 586,587..."

When the fraternity brother returned to the spot where he left the pledgee, he would ask, "how many bricks, Pledgee?"

"One thousand, three hundred and seventy-nine, Big Brother!"

"I'm sorry to hear you say that. I've been asking pledgees to count the bricks in this building face for the last two years and I know the exact number and it's more than 1,379. You better count them again." Invariably the Scroller would recount those bricks. The joke was that he would never be correct (or anyone else, for that matter). The count was always too short or too great. Yet, the real trick lay in outsmarting the Big Brother. Naturally, this was not immediately understood until quite some time had elapsed into the pledge period. Brothers could be very intimidat-

The Making of a Morehouse Man

ing and one took all of their commands seriously and literally. After all, we wanted to gain their acceptance. What we did not understand early on was that they wanted us to outsmart them. Their reasoning was that they did not want guys coming into their chapter who were not as sharp as they.

"Count the bricks in that wall, Pledgee."

"Yes, Big Brother!"

Then, because he was not going to stand there, doing nothing, while you counted bricks, he'd walk away. Then, if you had your wits about you, you would walk away and take a 30-minute nap or whatever. Later, you would return to the spot where he had left you supposedly counting bricks.

"How many bricks?"

"One thousand, eight hundred and sixty-four, Big Brother!" Depending upon his mood, he'd give you the line that would result in a recount or dismiss you. Yet, we discovered more often than not that if you did not return, remarkably, seldom anything would happen. He might remember to ask you how many bricks were in the wall, but secretly, if he returned to the spot he was glad that you were not stupid enough to be standing there counting bricks.

Pledging was an experience distinct from any I had had at that point in my life. It was a different type of learning. We were being taught in a somewhat systematic way to think on our feet in what was often a stressful environment. To some extent it was preparation to meet the stresses of the "real world" while having to perform in spite of them. The college itself was stressful enough. Added to this was the intimidation, fear and anxiety brought on by knowing these guys, to some degree, held the keys to your

Above Our Heads

entry into what was believed to be a tremendously exciting social dimension to the overall collegiate experience.

Paddling and other forms of hazing were outlawed at most colleges, even in the Sixties. This was true at Morehouse. Yet it was impossible to enforce this regulation. The pledgees did not tell. Pride and the "macho thing" of pledging prevented it. And fraternity brothers were never crazy enough to do acts of violence in the presence of anyone other than fraternity brothers and pledgees. For whatever reason, the majority of Kappas did not actively engage in physically violent behavior. While everyone that I know who underwent this experience condemns it for the absurd cruelty that it is, the threat of violence had the effect of making an utterly cohesive unit of the Scrollers in the pledge class.

We became as one person. If we did not, there were mind games that rather quickly led to this result.

"What's your name, Scroller?"

"Sir, Scroller James Hawes, Big Brother Reeves, Sir!"

Then asking Billy Gilbert his name, Gilbert would respond, predictably, "Sir, Billy Gilbert, Big Brother Reeves, Sir!"

"Whoa, little brother. Didn't Hawes say his name was Scroller James Hawes?"

"Yes Sir, Big Brother Reeves, Sir!"

"Aren't you supposed to be one Scroller?"

And, of course we were supposed to be one Scroller. One of the essential purposes of the pledge period was to build a community. "Yes Sir, Big Brother Reeves, Sir!"

"Then isn't your name 'Scroller James Hawes?'"

"Er, ah, yes sir, Big Brother Reeves!" When the question was

The Making of a Morehouse Man

put to the third Scroller this person was "Scroller James Hawes" as was the one after him, and the one following him and so on.

The five of us who were Freshmen had to leave the pledge class before induction because of the rule preventing freshmen from becoming members of a fraternity. While we could pledge as freshmen, we could only be inducted in our second year. I never understood the wisdom of this regulation, especially because of the risk to grade point averages. We had invested so much time into pledging that the one additional week that remained could not have materially altered our existence to our detriment. Still, we had to leave the "line" until we would become eligible for induction in the first semester of the sophomore year. Of the five freshmen that pledged that semester, only myself and James Hawes continued our pledge upon our return the following semester.

The first day that we were in the Scroller "doghouse" (so-called because pledges in the final week of the pledge process were called "dogs" by Big Brothers) was also to be our last day as pledges due to the college regulation against initiating freshmen. This day marked the first day of the last week of pledging that was also known as Hell Week. The Scroller who volunteered his room to serve as the doghouse either had no roommate, his roommate was also pledging (either Kappa or another fraternity) or his roommate agreed to switch rooms for this purpose.

On that last day, just as our Big Brothers were dismissing the freshmen from the "line" (pledge class), Big Brother Byron Glore, a recent graduate, burst into the room. Brothers, who might not have otherwise been present during the main portion of the pledge period, would show up out of nowhere, once word circulated that Hell Week had begun. Glore entered the room shouting and came up to one of my brothers who was a freshman and knocked the wind out of him. More angry than physically hurt, the pummeled Scroller, while recomposing himself, was offered profuse apologies from the Kappas who realized that he was wronged by this act since as of that moment he was no longer officially pledging. Once Glore recognized this, he too was effusive in his attempts at making amends. He seemed genuinely sorry for having touched the fellow in an offensive manner. Everyone, including the Scroller, was satisfied that this was a forgivable error, and, after a round of handshaking, the freshmen left the room.

The Making of a Morehouse Man

15

Morehouse College
Atlanta, Georgia

April 24, 1966

Dear Folks,

    I realize that I have not written in some time but I have been, so to speak, "caught-up in my `self.'" In other words, I've been trying to find out what kind of life I want to have; trying to find an identity; seeking to discover myself. I am constantly being exposed to a multiplicity of facets in life. I have become friends with intellects and rich "society" types and everything in between and cannot choose what life I would like best. I have of course been brought up with the idea that making money is the primary function of life. But now I have begun to question it. I ask myself if I am going to school so that I can be financially secure in life and by being so enjoy life. For that matter, is education a means to making money? I have come to realize that happiness is "life." I mean that if you are happy with what your doing no matter how much money it brings, then nothing else should matter. I believe that school is beautiful for the fact that it introduces you to the theories of life and exposes you to a few of its facets (practical experiences which are really typical of the world).

    I believe that if one goes through college with the misconceived notion that he will be a financial success upon graduating shouldn't go. I think I can gain more by attending college for learning's sake (and I don't mean learning about math as such but learning how to

Above Our Heads

reason and think through math). Of course I will do my best in practical application of the subject in class but my end will not be able to know how to work a problem for the sake of knowing how, but more so to learn how I arrived at the solution.

[THIS ENTIRE LETTER MAY BE A JUMBLED MASS OF THOUGHTS BUT I HAVE A LOT ON MY MIND ALL AT ONCE AND I WRITE AS I THINK OF AN IDEA
  (PROBLEM)].

Like I said before, I'm living in a period of indecision. I'm certain that if I'm happy in a livelihood there will be no regrets but I am not certain that what I plan to do (lawyer) will make me happy. I don't know if I should live as the prominent Negro lawyer possibly losing perspective with basic concepts of life (whatever they are) so engrossed with making money and becoming more "white," or if I should be the Black intellect who scorns the black bourgeoisie for trying to be like "whitey" and live a day-to-day existence happy with living by bare essentials but doing what I want (I don't know what that is). Or don't be conscious of a race-economic problem and just live a typically American middle-class existence—go to school, get a secure steady job upon graduation, marry, becoming economically secure, have children, work, work, work, die and leave the world "naked." The question remains, was the world (or anyone) effected by your existence? So you advanced yourself while living. Life was comfortable for you. Were you happy? How much time of your life did it take for you to achieve everything or anything you wanted? I'm a Negro but should that really matter when it comes time for me to start a livelihood?

The Making of a Morehouse Man

Whatever I do I know that I will have to practice it 100%. I'm afraid that I will have difficulty doing that. I enjoy the idea of having money whenever I want it. I also enjoy that carefree, non—obligatory (fantastic) life of let say the bearded intellect, from what I see. Of course both visions are through rose—colored glasses. I've never truly experienced either one. But I have been exposed to people wherein it is their natural habitat. I'm very confused and frustrated.

Anger at the federal government. They want soldiers so badly they are administering a qualification test to college students to weed out those too dumb to study but not to dumb to fight for their country. Some people will fail the test, become drafted, go to Viet Nam, get killed, who could have otherwise contributed something to this country by staying in school. I'm sure that when enough (too many) people pass the test another way will be devised to "recruit" soldiers.

Maybe it's best that a few college students are drafted. At least a great deal of their problems will be solved arising from the social conflicts present at educational institutions. I believe that there are more causes for emotional disturbance in this college (or any college, really) that I have ever been exposed to.

I'd like a girl who I could communicate comfortably. Someone with truly a mind. Not a silly thing. I haven't found one. Not a wife just a nice-looking (very attractive, so what) with some sense who can upset me and soothe me. And set me to thinking and help me to solve or come to a conclusion on some problem or situation. I've stopped searching. Not enough time.

I want to come home. To be frank not because it's so beautiful there but because it can be made beautiful. A challenge: I haven't had any sexual relations since I've been here and I regret it, I think that it's terrible. I've tried on several occasions to arrange something but something has always gone wrong. Either no girl and a beautiful situation or a beautiful girl and no situation. I've almost given up but dread self-persecution. Don't want to be a quitter. Then, too, I've always been told it was bad and not to be done. Conflict between id and superego and ego. Miserable existence. As if married life solves everything. I wonder why there are words like divorce, separation, desertion. Oh, well!

One more month of school. Hoping and working toward good grades. I'm almost becoming complacent because I'm sick of it all, but I know it's important and with these conflicting ideas I'm frustrated. Inspire.

Love,
Spencer

As the Spring semester was underway and the novelty of college life was waning, my thoughts began to dwell on philosophy of life issues. It seemed, though, that everyone in my class was wrestling with trying to make sense of the last few months. Maybe I was preoccupied with the larger issues because "ups" and "downs" occurred in such rapid succession that I could not focus.

I had had a successful pledge period but could not become a member of the fraternity until the following semester. I had made the Dean's List in my first semester but I did not believe that I was doing very well in the second. As was the case with most of my classmates, I was overly preoccupied with the idea of women, long since recognizing my apparent inability to attract one. It

The Making of a Morehouse Man

seemed as though school was becoming more difficult, not easier, with the passage of time and the increased experience.

We were all becoming philosophical about college and life afterwards. Yet, the one event that really had us on the edge of our seats was the Vietnam War.

The Selective Service System had made all of us register with our local draft boards when we reached the age of 18 years. If we could prove that we were college students, then we would receive the coveted 2-S draft status: not draftable until completion of college, departure from college before graduation or in the event of a national emergency. We were hearing the horror stories from all around the country that students unable to pay tuition would be forced to leave college and would become immediately a soldier in the United States Army. For a Black student with no college degree, this invariably meant service in the infantry on the front line. The chances of not coming back home loomed large.

The context for this war was unlike any that we had ever heard or read about. As Black men, we were particularly sensitive to the fact that we were being compelled to fight against enemies of color. While it was true that this same demand was made upon Black GIs in the Korean War, race consciousness had taken on a broader level of understanding. As Black men, we were beginning to see ourselves in solidarity with men and women of every color: brown, black, red and yellow. We began to realize that it was as illogical to kill the Vietnamese as it was to believe that white people looked upon us as their brothers and comrades in arms, fighting together to make the world safe for democracy. The truth in America for us was that democracy was not a reality for people of color who were U.S. citizens. This could be easily tested by get-

Above Our Heads

ting in a car and driving 10 miles beyond the city limits of Atlanta in any direction. Stop at a gas station where a white attendant half your age might be working, and one would not be surprised to be greeted with "Boy, how much gas do you want today?"

It was because we were constantly bombarded with these conflicting messages that caused confusion, depression and an anxiousness about our purposes in life, both individually and collectively. When I finished my time in the Scrollers Club, though I had yet to be initiated into Kappa, I felt an incredible pressure lifted. I was given some breathing room. The pledge period ended just before the spring break. I was invited by Samuel Jennings, then a junior and one of my Big Brothers, to travel to Orlando, Florida for the break. I had always heard of college kids going to Florida at this time of the year. Generally, it would be to Ft. Lauderdale. In the early part of the Sixties, this town in south Florida had been popularized in a movie titled "Where the Boys Are," which depicted hoards of collegians converging upon this beachfront resort for wild nights and days of fun and cavorting. Orlando was even better.

Sam and I arrived in Orlando and were met at the airport by another Floridian and Morehouse Kappa, Ralph Armstead. Since Sam and Ralph grew up in this town, they knew all kinds of people. It was one of the best vacations, primarily due to its being my first time away from the parental supervision of home and the regimen of college. Though not yet an adult, I was being treated like one and for the entire time felt like one.

Sam and Ralph had a female friend who lived in Orlando they had known from childhood. She went by the nickname "Dump" and was an incredibly exciting personality. Even though she lived with her mother in a lovely home, she acted as though she lived alone as she could come and go as she pleased and entertained in her home as an adult might. Let me hasten to add that I was never intimate with Dump nor she with anyone else in my presence, but she had a self-assured style that caused her to appear older than she actually was. It was invigorating, liberating to be in her company. I began to feel as if I, too, could do anything. To some extent this experience exceeded my "Fort Lauderdale-cum-'Where the Boys Are'" fantasy of the college spring break. Unlike the childish pranks and 20 people sharing a motel room, so typical of the Lauderdale episodes, we lived comfortably at Sam's mother's home, but spent nights at friends' homes as we wanted.

One day Dump suggested that we go to Daytona Beach, where she had been a student at Bethune-Cookman College until she dropped out the year earlier. I never saw the college. Her plan was to drive along the beach. Actually, we drove in her Volkswagen on the beach. I had never driven a car on a public beach, much less to speed on one. As I have mentioned, being around Dump was a liberating experience. I enjoyed being with a wonderfully sensuous and exciting woman without giving in to libidinous urges. This was a difficult lesson to learn, as I was so inexperienced in affairs of the heart. To find satisfaction through the enjoyment of a platonic friendship with a lovely female was a triumph over the raging hormones of an 18-year-old male.

16

Breckenridge House

May 19, 1966

Dear Folks,

 My exams will be completed on May 26. On May 27, 28, 29 is the "Newport Jazz Festival" in Atlanta. I may stay a few days. Just one or two) for that depending upon how well I enjoy it. On May 31 from 2 A.M. to 6 A.M. is the Kappa Dawn Dance (a dance given early in the morning,, the day before graduation, hence dawn dance, by Kappa Alpha Psi Fraternity, Inc.) Of course, even though I am not yet a Kappa I will still be admitted free. I am doubtful, however, as to whether or not I want to attend because coming home early would be nice (I suppose; but the kids wouldn't be back from school, would they?)

 I would love to write George but in all the letters I receive from you requesting me to do so you never give an address.

 I know for sure that I will be home no later than June 1. If I decide not to go to the Kappa Dawn Dance (or if you write back and tell me that you don't want me to attend) then I will be home on May 29. I am trying to get my own fare back home. I will no doubt fly. The experience was quite enjoyable when I flew to Florida and back for Easter. As you know Delta and Eastern Airlines have incorporated the 12-21 Plan. It means for students to fly anywhere for (one-half) the usual price. If I go by plane I will get a one—way ticket, however, if you insist I go home via train then that is what I will do.

The Making of a Morehouse Man

Yes, I received the check and your letters. If I get another "B" average I will immediately grab the prize of $100 (for being on the honor roll twice in a row) and depart from here for good. If I'm still interested in Kappa I may come back for the 1st semester of sophomore year to be initiated.

I believe I want to go to a white school with more challenge (Antioch, for instance) or either Lincoln University in Pennsylvania. Morehouse has lost any academic atmosphere it once had and the party. Then again if I don't get the "B" average I'll be back and stay until I do only so that I may transfer. Trigonometry (Transcendental Functions) is given me a rough time. My average: 55. If I don't get at least an 85 on the final then I will get a grade of "D" or below. I'm studying it everyday (and I'm saying that to rationalize any grade I may receive) I will take the course again if disaster confronts me!

How's dad's dog, pepper, doing? Have Marvin and Billy been wearing their Morehouse T-shirts. Will try to get some sweatshirts.

Love,
Spencer

Fortunately, I did not get the "B" average that I believed would have motivated me to transfer from Morehouse. Actually, I was disappointed. The success of the first semester went to my head. I felt that I did not have to work as hard the second semester. I didn't and it showed. Yet, Morehouse was for me a complicated place. Perhaps the first year of college, Anywhere, USA, is a difficult experience. But I was at Morehouse and this was my experience.

ABOVE OUR HEADS

The fact of the matter was that, far from losing any of its academic challenge, Morehouse was simply challenging in a variety of ways, not the least of which was academic. I was simply worn out from juggling the demands of classwork and social life. While Lincoln University, another Black and male college, and Antioch were fine schools, they were probably no more challenging than Morehouse. People often believed that a Black college campus was an inadequate place to prepare for life in the real world. There was the sense that, without the interplay between the nation's majority culture and students of color, that Blacks would not be able to compete with whites after graduation. What was not fully appreciated was the notion that Morehouse and a few other predominately Black colleges possessed two powerful abilities: nurturing the development of the total person and creating the sense that one must pursue graduate and/or professional school after graduation. The first, once completed, enabled the fulfillment of the second.

From a copy of the MOREHOUSE COLLEGE BULLETIN of the period, a recital of the "Aims" should serve to demonstrate how the college sought to fulfill its objective in developing the total person:

"1. To develop his character.
2. To develop and train his mental aptitude.
3. To acquire scholarly habits of work and study.
4. To acquire the ability to read understandingly and to express himself intelligently.
5. To obtain a broad background in the arts and sciences for a life career.
6. To understand the nature of man and his relation to the physical universe.
7. To cultivate an appreciation for the cultural and

The Making of a Morehouse Man

spiritual qualities of life.
8. To understand and interpret constructively, current social and economic problems.

"In achieving these ends, the College seeks to combine instructional and extracurricular activities to the extent that the student will have an opportunity to display initiative, display expression, acquire greater confidence in himself, and to gain a type of experience which will enable him, as a citizen, to furnish a quality of leadership that will be constructive and far-seeing."

During this first year it was evident that the school could not, nor sought to, shelter its students from the realities of life beyond the campus. Its location in the middle of working-class Black Atlanta was continuing evidence of its complete identity with Black America. The school was intrinsically entwined into the total community in which Black people had their being. Its graduates often came from Atlanta's affluence and certainly almost always served to perpetuate it. Yet, the school was a beacon of hope for Atlanta's Black underclass. A day would not go by when neighborhood boys (and it was always only boys, since girls would never be admitted as students) would fail to be a presence on campus, emulating us and often looking for ways to become a part of us. These young fellows, while in high school (and some in grade school), wished more than ever to become students here. Those of us who were open to their presence let them do odd jobs for us as a way of encouraging their dreams. Many of these kids, who came from families where no one had gone to college, eventually gained acceptance to Morehouse.

At some point the guys in Unit 5 began seeing themselves as

Above Our Heads

something akin to a fraternal organization. Like the other freshman groupings, we continued to hang out together, even sitting together for meals in the Alvin H. Lane Dining Room, the college's cafeteria. In doing this, we emulated the fraternities. On special occasions, fraternities would dress their tables in tablecloths representative of the fraternity's colors. After seeing this a couple of times, someone suggested that we should have colors. Another, a name. One day, six of us gathered together in Clarence Yokely's room (Hugh Dash, myself, George Watson, Robert Gholdston, James Wells and Yokely) and began throwing out names to one another: the Cavaliers, the Esquires and so on. We tried out a few Greek letter combinations, considering momentarily becoming part of either Groove Phi Groove or Wine Psi Phi, organizations that had begun to spring up all across Black College America. No one was satisfied. Then someone thought aloud: why not name the building? This seemed to strike a nerve with everyone. No one had liked the fact that our building, though located in Quarles Court (named for The Rev. Frank Quarles, the first pastor of historic Friendship Baptist Church, where Morehouse was located after its founding in Augusta, Georgia), was simply named Unit 5.

Someone grabbed a dictionary and began thumbing through it looking for what was the "proper" name for us (read: *highfalutin'*). When the name John Cabell Breckinridge was uttered, everyone took note. It did not matter that he was the vice-president of the United States just before the Civil War who later became a confederate general. We simply liked the sound. Breckinridge. So we became Breckinridge House after trying out the name on all the other residents. For whatever reasons, while

The Making of a Morehouse Man

curiosity was high among all who learned of this occurrence, no one ever did any research to find out who Breckinridge was or why Breckinridge was chosen. Like the fraternities, with all of their mystery and sworn oaths, this was to be our first secret.

The colors became light blue and black. The first day that we decorated our section of the dining room with similarly colored table cloths, it created quite a stir. It was a Sunday, and while everyone had to wear jackets and ties to Sunday luncheon, everyone was dressed particularly well that day and behaved superbly at meal. Most Sundays, in protest against the dress code, guys would wear plaid trousers, striped coats with outlandish polka dot ties. Not so the Breckinridge crew. Dark suits, white or blue shirts and appropriately matching ties. People, of course, approached our table asking a hundred questions, to which they received evasive replies. It was not until the sign was made that the school really took us seriously.

I was assigned the task of creating a sign befitting our emerging prominence on campus. Some of them had seen the Bacardi Rum label I had crafted for Joe Somerville and believed that I had the capacity to carry out this task. I secured a piece of rectangular plywood about three feet by five and painted the name Breckinridge in a "Black-letter" type face. Then, I painted the border in alternating colors of black and light blue. After this dried, I added several coats of shellac to weatherproof it. Once completed, we proudly hung the sign from the roof of the porch at the entrance to the building.

It did not take long for Robert West, the director of housing to learn that one of "his" buildings had been "defaced" by the hanging of an inappropriate and unauthorized sign declaring a change in the name of the building. Students in other settings, fueled by envy, had apparently reported us to him. Yet, there were a number of students not in our building who supported our actions. When President Benjamin Mays got involved in the discussion, things really became interesting. Mr. West was not allowed to remove the sign. Word had gotten to Dr. Mays even before it was hung on the building that the fellows in Unit 5 had banded together and were even taking meals together in the dining room. Though this was not unusual, what was out of the ordinary was the proper decorum by which we conducted ourselves when we were at table.

President Mays reasoned that, if a group of freshmen were able to set an example for the entire resident student body, then why begrudge them the use of their sign? It only seemed to instill pride in the property, thereby protecting it from the occasional abuses some residences received. So for most of the second semester we were Breckinridge and scored considerable points with students and administrators alike. Yet Robert West would be closely watching.

Almost as soon as I left the campus Chicago-bound, I felt homesick - that is, homesick for Morehouse. I knew that despite all the "stuff" that had been thrown at me, there was no place where I would rather be. I had grown so much in just nine months that I had actually become a new person. The institution, with its faculty, staff and incredible student body, had revealed a different way for me to perceive the world.

The most frightening factor regarding leaving school was in returning home where an "infantalization" process was sure to await. I was afraid that the experience of almost a year of living

The Making of a Morehouse Man

as an adult would be automatically exchanged for a childlike re-existence in my parent's home. To some extent my fears were not unfounded. I was after all a "guest" in my parent's home and was required to abide by the rules of their house. At Morehouse I was my own person; at my parent's house, I marched to their beat. But after the first year, they recognized too that I had matured somewhat and maybe was entitled to a relaxation of the strict code that continued to guide the behavior of my two younger brothers.

Benjamin and Sadie Mays

Spencer C. Gibbs

Robert Cross

Typical room in The Units

Dean Brazeal, Charles West, Joseph Somerville,
E. B. Williams and Robert Tucker

Duane Jackson

Fr. Warren Scott

George Watson

Haywood Hodge

Barry Gaither, Spelman student, E. J. Brisker and Walter Dancy standing in fornt of Canterbury House

Morehouse/Spelman students in football stadium

Student Court

Track Team Leaders: (l-r) - Edgar Thomas, Raines Carrol and Stephen Johnson

James Hawes

Dr. Melvin Dow Kennedy

Marching Tigers

Kappas in 1967 l-r: Charles Jackson, James Tyler, David Reeves, Sandford Bishop, Marvin D. Raines, Richard Hudlin, C. Vernon Mason, Isaac Joe, Mark Hill and Leon Collins

Robert W. West

Psi Chapter of Omega Psi Phi in 1966

Larry Burt

Phi Lambdas (Carl Bowman is standing fourth from left)

Alpha Phi Alpha (Eric Mitchell is standing directly below the words "Alpha Rho;" Sam Wilder is on left holding sign.)

Chi Chapter of Phi Beta Sigma in 1966, (John Houser, a Bennet Hall buddy, is seated second from right)

Fall Line 1966 (l-r): Donald Hense, Karl Merritt, Gibbs, James Hawes

Kappa brother Charles Cabbage is #32

Dr. Benjamin E. Mays
says farewell

Benjamin E. Mays passing Presidential Robe to
Hugh M. Gloster who suceeded Mays as President
of Morehouse College, Februrary 17, 1968

Above Our Heads

Kappas in 1968 (l-r standing): James Hawes, Michael Gray, Sanford Bishop, Karl Merritt, Eric Smith, Jon Browne, Albert T. Smith, Donald Hense, Spencer Gibbs, Richard Hudlin, Robert Duncan, Glen Taylor, Theodric Harrell, Holding sign: James Somerville (left) and John McCottrell in front of Kappa Court

Morehouse Kappas and Spelman sweethearts

Swim Team: Top Row - Robert Garcia, Jospeh Ruscito, Clarence Grisham, Michael Clark, Juan Lieba, Sidney Brooks, Isaiah B. King Bottom Row - Lambert Green, Elias Burton, John T. Franks, James Fannin, Wigberto Cintron, Richard Allen and Michael Davis

Pi Brothers in 1969 in front of Kappa Chapter House (Victor wright's MGB-GT balances off the following brothers - l-r, bottom row: Roderick Pettigrew, John McCottrell, Eric Smith, Roland H. Crowder, Michael Gray, Victor Wright, Martin Bryant, Jimmie Millhouse, Larry Dingle, Calvin O. Butts III, Thomas Woodhouse, Donald L. Hense and James Dennis. l-r, top row: Orlando Protho, Robert Kennedy, Reginald E. Pierce, James B. Hawkins, James Somerville, Gibbs, Calvin Calhoun, John H. "Cochise" Smith, Curtis Hariss, H. Randolph Scott II, James Brown and Jon Browne)

The King comes home

The streets completely filled with King mourners

Social and Cultural Affairs Committee, (l-rr): Kenzil Sumney, Herman Outlaw, Theodric Harrell, Clark White, Roman Williams, Malcolm Beech (chairman), Gregory Brown, Elliot Malone, Charles Allen and Samuel L. Jackson

Nelson Taylor, 1968-69 SGA President

Robert DeLeon, Editor-in-Chief, 1968 Torch

Neal "Bama" Robinson

Kappas in 1966: clockwise beginning in front - Joseph Somerville, Leon Collins, Ralph Armstead, David Reeves, C. Vernon Mason, Charles Cabbage, James Tyler, Victor Wright, Nelson Taylor, Robert Brown, Samuel Jennings and Samuel Williams

Edward Long

Ronald DeVerges

Pan Hellenic Council: Hense (2nd from left lower row) Gibbs (top row far left), Jimmie Millhouse (3rd from right, lower row), all Kappas

Above Our Heads

The Making of a Morehouse Man

YEAR TWO

Finally an Upperclassman

"Dear Old Morehouse, dear old Morehouse,
We have pledged our lives to thee.
And we'll ever, yea forever
Give ourselves in loyalty.

"True forever, true forever
To old Morehouse may we be;
So to bind each son the other
Into ties more brotherly.

"Holy Spirit, Holy Spirit,
Make us steadfast, honest, true;
To old Morehouse, and her ideals,
And in all things that we do."

The Morehouse College Alma Mater

Above Our Heads

The Making of a Morehouse Man

1

Sept. 27, 1966

Dear Folks,

The trip down was not bad. I arrived in Atlanta at 11:00 AM Sunday. Fortunately, I met a few people that attend school in Atlanta that made the trip enjoyable. I managed to get a room with little trouble. My roommates are James Hawes from Elberton, Georgia, the fellow I told you about who pledged with me, and a senior named Eric Mitchell from Virginia who is A Phi A.

My address is:
Spencer Gibbs
Box 299
Morehouse Coll.
Atlanta, Ga.

This year is the first year that mailboxes have been issued to undergrads at Morehouse.

My course load is:

101 Physical Science 3 hrs Dr. Neff from Harvard
251 Humanities II 3 hrs Dr. Campbell, Ph.D. U. of Chi.
252 French 2nd sem. 4 hrs Mr. Dillard, M.A. La Sorbonne
251 Sociology 3 hrs Mr. Chivers, M.A. from New York U.
251 Political Science 3 hrs Dr. Johnson, Ph.D. Harvard
251 Phys. Educ. 1 hr P.E. Staff one Ph.D., rest Masters

---
17 hrs

Above Our Heads

  I got my job at the library. For the time being I am financially secure. I'm not certain when fraternity intends to initiate us, will inform you when fateful day arises.

            Love,
            Spencer

It was a rainy, overcast day in Atlanta when I arrived by cab to the campus from the Southern Pacific Railroad Station. The place never looked better. It seemed as though all my first-year worries were nothing more than faded memories. I was now an upperclassman. It felt different. As I walked about the campus, I smiled inwardly at this new crop of Crabgrass. Though I was only a year older than most of them, they looked so young and naive, especially by the way in which they regarded us. I do not believe that we did anything that was purposely designed to elicit their awe, but there was on their part a decidedly admiring look on their faces as they looked upon those of us returning as upperclassmen.

  There is no way of knowing for certain whether or not the ease with which I was able to get a room assignment had to do with the fact of my being a sophomore. Still, I recall passing the long line of freshmen who had been waiting to be assigned rooms before I had arrived to the housing office and walking to my quarters, key in hand, leaving them still hoping to acquire a room before sunset.

  James Hawes and I had decided to get a room together in Unit One. We applied for and received the large second floor room. We believed that it would be ours without any additional roommates.

The Making of a Morehouse Man

It was felt that rooming together would facilitate our working together as we were the only ones who had pledged Kappa in the previous semester and who intended on becoming initiated this semester. When we arrived, Eric was already unpacked and lying upon the bunk that was to be his.

Eric Mitchell was a tall Virginian who looked more white than Black. He was a business major and extremely smart. This year he was to serve his chapter of Alpha Phi Alpha Fraternity as its President. So, he was also a campus leader. During our first year, guys like Eric were far removed from us, largely because freshmen who were not on athletic teams lived in separate dorms from upperclassmen. Now, because Hawes and I were upperclassmen, sophomores, juniors and seniors might find themselves living together without regard to class.

Life with Eric was immediately demythologizing. While Eric presented this cool, confident public posture, we discovered that he had the same fears and anxieties as all the rest of us. For him they could have been compounded with the fact that after this year he would be leaving the comfortable familiarity of Morehouse and moving on to the unpredictability of graduate school.

Eric was going steady with a beautiful, tall woman who could have easily been a fashion model, had she not been a full-time senior at Spelman. This year she was to become the Sweetheart of Alpha during Eric's tenure as president of the chapter. They were to become married upon graduation.

I thought it was going to be hell living with this prima donna-type personality. At first Eric tried us. Hawes and I were pretty self-assured and could resist his attempts at putting us in our place. After all, he was a graduating senior and we still had three years to go. The factor that evened us out was the advent into our threesome of Brother Larry Burt.

Burt was a junior from Detroit. Larry was Eric's foil. Where Hawes and I at first may have been hesitant to volley one of Eric's flippant remarks with our own rejoinder, Larry was without peer in his ability to level Eric with his own brand of verbal one upmanship. For Larry was as streetwise as Eric was accomplished in the classroom. Neither was anybody's dummy, but while Eric seemed to have been raised in the lap of patrician luxury, Larry Burt had the hard edge typical of an adolescent life lived in a serious urban atmosphere.

Even though we were two Southerners and two Northerners, there were no alliances based upon region. As a matter of fact, after the first few days we all got along rather well. We became a sort of community center, perhaps because there were four very distinctive personalities living in one room who appealed to a broad range of our peers in the college. As a result, we got to know one another's friends who, in many instances, became each other's friends. The people I met during this time, as a result of my diverse roommates, were persons who I might never have sought out as friends on my own.

The entire student body was enormously proud of the faculty we were privileged to have teach us. I had to write my parents simply to let them know of the enviable credentials of my professors. Even more amazing was that, during this semester, only my physical science teacher, Professor Samuel H. Neff, had not received an undergraduate degree from Morehouse.

Finley Campbell, a professor of English, was a brilliant schol-

The Making of a Morehouse Man

ar and teacher. Campbell deepened my appreciation for literature and my skills in literary analysis. He was the one who first interpreted for me the concept of "the Christian" as one who is Christ-like. He then quickly went on to explain that this was the dilemma of the Christian: the follower was to attempt to live a life like Christ with the full knowledge that this was utterly impossible. I remember seeing Finley in the pulpit of the Sale Hall Chapel giving a sermon at one of our mandatory thrice weekly chapel services. It was also the first time I had ever seen a "preacher" (Finley was knowledgeable about the scriptures though not an ordained minister) utilize a "visual" sermon illustration. While making a point about the superficiality of life, he removed his robe and revealed the ragged clothing of a bum. His point was that it is much more important who a person is on the inside than what they appear to be by the clothes they wear.

Tobe Johnson was a no-nonsense professor of political science. He was one of those who caused me to think long and hard before electing to become a political science minor. Yet, I never felt adequate to the task, as Johnson had a way of being terribly demanding. I remember at a football game during half-time when we all rushed to the lavatories. Dr. Johnson was at a urinal when a senior student occupied an adjoining one. Said the student: "I'm going to kick your ass on the final, Tobe."

Though the student was obviously drunk, Professor Johnson calmly responded: "I hope you do, son, I hope you do." And that was all. I couldn't believe my ears, but I came to discover that this was not an altogether unusual exchange between students and the Morehouse faculty. Johnson knew that he was respected and that he brought a great deal of pressure and anxiety to the persons

Above Our Heads

who were majors in Political Science. Yet, this apparent faculty tolerance for student flippancy/anger was accommodated because of the unusual promise that most Morehouse students displayed for becoming leaders in the world community.

Mr. Walter Chivers, one of the oldest, longest tenured members of the faculty, was affectionately known as Pop Chivers. His wife, Dr. Naomi Chivers, was at this time the dean of Spelman College and was herself a legend at the women's school. Morris Dillard and James Haines shared with Campbell, Chivers and Johnson the distinction of having graduated Morehouse. Samuel Neff, a physicist, who did his undergraduate work at Pomona College in California completed my roster of instructors.

ID
2

Box 299   Oct. 10, 1966

Dear Folks,

    I'm very sorry if I appeared to be selfish in my last letter. I will try to consider your feelings and be more thoughtful when writing to you. I know that burdening you with a hodge-podge of inconsistent ideas does the three of us no good.
    I'm glad that you wrote what you did, Dad. I realize that things are only as bad as you make them. I guess I was just in a psychological slump that day. Momma, I don't want you to worry. I am doing fine. My roommates Eric and James, are quite enjoyable fellows to live with.
    I resolved that when the time comes that I will finish pledging. For this will only be another example of my running away from a situation. I like Morehouse and the fellows. I had stated that it was a few of the men in the fraternity that went against my grain, but I'm certain that even if I never truly like them that I will learn to understand them and live with them in a tolerable climate.
    I would appreciate a "box" at this time. I don't want to pressure you I know that your time is well-spent, but I had the understanding before I left that you would send one about a month after I got here.
    Homecoming is on the 12th of November (the weekend of the 12th). Are you coming? I won't be able to go anywhere for Thanksgiving holiday as it is only one day (Thursday is Thanksgiving, 8:00 AM Friday classes will be in session).

Above Our Heads

If you can find those pictures of some "girl friends" of mine in my desk drawer, please send them. They will be inside of the pink eyeglass case.

Love,
Spencer

While I had returned to the college an upperclassman, some of the doubts of the previous year continued to plague me. A major item was the fact that I had yet to complete the pledge period for membership into Kappa Alpha Psi. James Hawes and I were the only two of the previous semester's pledge line who did not "go over." We thought that since we had gone the distance leading up to Hell Week that we would automatically be accorded entry into the fraternity with no problem. We quickly discovered how wrong we were.

Shortly after the semester got underway, fraternities began their recruitment efforts for new members. As always, Kappa took an extremely nonchalant posture, never aggressively seeking anyone. Their attitude was: "If you are interested, we will consider you for membership." This appealed to me. They were very comfortable with themselves. So, when only two persons enrolled in the Scrollers Club, I was not surprised or dismayed. I reasoned that Kappa was not for everyone, Thank God! Yet, as the pledge period went on, Hawes and I were beginning to receive daily pressure to rejoin the pledge club. We protested. It was our understanding that we would only return to the Scrollers Club at the beginning of Hell Week, the last week of the pledge period known also as the probationary period, leading to initiation. The Brothers argued that we needed to become part of the two who were already

The Making of a Morehouse Man

pledging, to solidify the fraternal bond with them. It was a compelling argument that caused us to strike a compromise: we returned to the "line" two weeks before initiation instead of one.

Personally, however, when I found myself agreeing to this arrangement, I felt betrayed. I argued with myself that I was again giving in to the machinations of life at Morehouse and not taking charge. As I opened up to my Big Brothers, some of whom I could talk to honestly, with this concern, they reasoned that they did not have to allow us entry back into the pledge club, regardless of the agreements of the previous semester. Once we agreed with their position, we were allowed to proceed with the semester's other pressures with one less from them.

Donald Hense and Karl Merritt were the two members of the 1966 pledge class or what was known as the fall line. Pledges (or pledgees) would have to walk in a single file whenever they walked together. Therefore, the pledge club of every fraternity was referred to as a line. Hense was from St. Louis, Missouri and was considerably older than most of the students at the college. Merritt was from Camilla, Georgia and though he entered Morehouse as a freshman with me, I had not made his acquaintance before this time. All four of us were members of the sophomore class, so, as classmates as well as line brothers, we were poised to form a close bond with one another. Hawes and I had had the earlier experience of pledging with 13 other guys during the Spring of '66, eight of whom were now our Big Brothers. He, I and they became very close even though Hawes and I initially approached Hense and Merritt more as strangers than as our pledge brothers. This, however, would quickly change.

Within hours of our joining Merritt and Hense "on line," our

Above Our Heads

former pledge brothers, now neophytes to Kappa, regarded us as outsiders. I don't believe that they treated us badly, they just did not give us the insider's welcome that we believed it was our right to receive, having gone through a common bonding experience.

One of the more important events that was designed to help us bond to one another while simultaneously separating ourselves from our former pledge class was the Greek show. It was a public performance staged by each fraternity's line involving an exhibition of intricately choreographed precision dance/step/marching movements. It was a way of impressing the community, making the fraternity look good and ingratiating ourselves with our big brothers. These events were also called step shows because the routines were dominated by the line's ability to entertain simply by displaying intricate footwork much like the military's version of close order drill. Often, the success of a line's proficiency at executing what was nothing less than performance art served as a marketing tool for others considering fraternal affiliation. Women also loved these shows immensely and, therefore, another pressure was added to the pledge's life: Don't shame the fraternity.

In our first Scroller pledge class we provided a combination of traditional step show with vocal art. Unlike the other pledge clubs, at the direction of our creative Dean of Pledges, C. Vernon "Bop" Mason, we emphasized the vocal gifts of the line over the typically crowd-pleasing step show normally presented and given by absolutely everyone else. After assessing our abilities, Mason believed (and I think correctly) that we could not compete with the other lines' stepping techniques. So, we practiced singing and discovered that we could do that well. Very well.

The Making of a Morehouse Man

On a beautiful spring day in 1966, the Scrollers Club of Pi Chapter marched over to Spelman College to perform. Having rehearsed our "number" until Bop was satisfied, we marched with confidence to the Yard. We waited until a substantial crowd had gathered and then began to perform an intricate pattern of "steps." No sooner than we had started, we stopped, but not before assembling ourselves in a semi-circle facing our audience of Spelman women. The next thing I knew, yet just as we had planned it, I opened my mouth and out came the opening line of "Why Do Fools Fall In Love?" My brothers sang the most incredible background to my sincere but feeble efforts and that is what got us over that day. I mean it really got us over. We were asked to sing encores. And we did. Our big brothers loved it, not really believing that we were as successful as we seemed to be. Women swooned. It could have been an act but I remember seeing some of these ladies having to be lifted off the ground. After what seemed at first to be an eternity, and soon felt like an instant what with all of the adulation we were receiving, we marched back to Morehouse and to the critical assessments of the chapter. Truth be told, we knew that we had "turned Spelman out," our slang for "made an enormous impression." Yet, we also knew that these men were not quick to bestow compliments.

When we returned to the "doghouse," we were shocked by their reaction. They loved us! More congenial backslapping and hugs I had never felt. And then the announcement was made that the freshmen would have to leave the line because of the College's rule preventing their initiation. A real roller coaster of an experience.

Hazing was still alive and well at Pi Chapter and the fact that

Above Our Heads

this was an all-male college made hazing particularly frightening. Though many of our classes experienced the presence of a small number of female students who took courses in their major that were not offered at Spelman, life at Morehouse, particularly during the evening hours, was exclusively a male environment. There did not exist that "buffering" element the presence of women provided that would stay the hand or fist that would invariably find its target on your arms, torso or worse. Most of the time we were merely the butt of crude jokes heaped upon us unmercifully by our tormentors, the members of the chapter. Yet, being a student in an educational complex with five other institutions of higher learning, we were fair game for Kappas wherever they matriculated. Our own chapter's big brothers, on rare occasions, would turn to violent forms of hazing, while "protecting" us from their brothers in neighboring Clark College, Morris Brown College and Atlanta University, the graduate school. Let me just state here that the period calls to mind the maxim "What doesn't kill you, can only make you stronger." We were quickly becoming decidedly stronger.

With this knowledge and experience, Hawes and I were compelled to join Merritt and Hense and undergo a second experience of Greek shows. This time, it was decidedly more pedestrian than the first time around. Given the fact that Hense was older than the other three of us, the chapter was faced with the problem of pulling something off that would not cause the line to look too ridiculous and compromise the image of the chapter as well. We could not do a singing show, since that had been performed by the line in the last semester. Mason had to come up with something new.

The Making of a Morehouse Man

I'm sure it was Hense's idea, but this will never be provable. We staged a scene out of some 1930's costumed comedy in which the four of us, dressed in tails, were chauffeured to Spelman in a limousine and driven to the dormitory to collect our formally attired "dates." They then returned with us to the limo and drove to a second location on campus. Once there, our big brothers, dressed as waiters, escorted us to outdoor "dining tables" where we acted as though we were ordering a meal.

This took place in December, 1966. It was cold, even though we were in Atlanta. The eight of us made the best of it (I realized why Hawes, Hense, Merritt and I were there, but those women...), acting as though we were seated in the most elegant restaurant imaginable. Thankfully, our big brothers provided champagne, for which the ladies were highly appreciative, since they were dressed as though they were sitting indoors instead of outside in 50 degree weather. They drank quite a bit more than us and seemed to enjoy every moment of our skit, which by the way was totally pantomimed without one audible expression. To my surprise, we were a hit.

While we all experienced a high degree of discomfort during the pledge period, entry into the fraternity was a crowning achievement in our lives. Upon becoming new initiates (or neophytes as the most recent members are called), the same guys that had been making our lives miserable, received us like long-lost relatives. I felt like the prodigal son must have felt. I was embraced, I was cherished, I was regarded as an equal (now suddenly, with them, superior to all other mortals). And it felt great! We gathered arm-in-arm in the parking lot in front of Quarles Court, and sang the fraternity hymn. There was loud and raucous merriment

Above Our Heads

and even a few tears of joy were shed. And, yes, on that night there was a fatted calf: We had a huge banquet attended by present and past members of Pi Chapter. The brothers had earlier arranged for us to be feted at a Hunter Street restaurant known simply as Williams Tavern. We marched from campus to the restaurant several blocks away, in a single file down the middle of the street, using the yellow line as a guide. We had a private room in a lackluster place that seemed to the Fall Line of '66 like the Taj Mahal. We ate and drank and sang and laughed and had simply one of the best times that I can recall in my then very young life.

The Making of a Morehouse Man

3

Oct. 29, 1966

Dear Folks,

I have received the books. I know the importance of letting you know about receiving the articles you send and will try in the future to be more punctual in replying to your letters.

Mr. Mosely's death comes as a shock of course but then too I'm positive, to a degree, that the situation next door has not become worse. At first you say the members are quiet and then you couple the preceding information with the shooting of Mr. Wiley. What more is necessary? Is Mr. Wiley recovering nicely?

I haven't met Jefferson T. Ware as yet. Even though the school is small it is often difficult to find someone.

I cannot give you any information on my academic progress as one day I will do very well and the next fall slightly. At first Humanities was giving me increasing difficulty but I am getting that under control.

In other words, if I don't write neither will you. That appears to be a tragic situation, therefore I will attempt to keep things at a happy medium. Of course you will realize that I have no great affinity towards letter-writing but I will try to write more often.

Homecoming is on the weekend of November 12. Based on my experiences last year the Homecoming will be filled with activities of a variety: lectures, football games, parties, school dances, banquets, etc. You may procure a room at a number of fine hotels in Atlanta. Maybe you might want to contact the Cross family or the Jackson's. They could probably tell you more.

The nearest phone to me is 753-9343; the area code is 404. I've answered all desired questions. If there is anything you want to know just let me know.

Love,
Spencer

My parents were supplying their own brand of pressure to life at Morehouse. I thought that by going to a place as far away from Chicago as Atlanta that I would be out of their tenacious hold. Physically, of course, this was true. I had lived the entire previous year as close to the life of an adult as an 18-year-old can live. Yet, I had underestimated (if I had given any thought to it at all) the tremendous psychological hold parents with the best of interests can maintain over their children.

What I did not realize then was that college was not just a context in which I was expected to mature. My college years were also the occasion for enormous adjustment problems for my parents. This was a novel experience for all of us: Before the previous year I had never lived away from home and they had never had one of their children not living with them. They were anxious about what was going on with me in ways I may never know. So they insisted on hearing from me. Letter-writing was the means of choice since the costs of using the telephone could have become prohibitive if I had viewed it as a standard means to communicate. I wasn't going to pay for it and it became quickly obvious that they were not desirous of doing so when the operator announced that their son was calling collect from Atlanta followed by my appeal for money.

They got used to my letters. After a time I came to enjoy writing because I found that I could write to them about things that I had trouble speaking to them about. It also helped to affirm my emerging adulthood. In letters, I could communicate as a person and not simply as Bobby and Eththelle's little boy. But, as importantly, they were compelled to read my communications if they wanted to know what was going on with me. They lost the capacity of disregarding me or arguing with each statement that I might make.

This forced us all to grow. Letter-writing became a type of communication that happens between people who cannot speak face to face about difficult or emotional topics without becoming hysterical. Letter-writing allowed us to reason together when verbal communication simply could not sustain the emotional burden that was carried by both sides. I even discovered that I felt one way when I received a typed letter than when I received one-handwritten from either parent. The handwritten letter generated a warmth that was not evident in the often terse typed communication I might receive from my "concerned" parents.

Above Our Heads

4

Nov. 22, 1966

Dear Folks,

I started answering your letter as soon as I received the birthday card and the money, but I couldn't finish at that time and lost it. Now that I am alone in my room (which is not often) I remembered I hadn't answered. When you receive this letter I will be finishing up my pledge period. I will need about $50 for I have saved $30 already. If you still want to give me your pin I will be more than happy to accept it. I don't know the exact amount of initiation but that amount (our combined totals) should cover the cost.

My grade predictions for the half semester are as follows:

Hrs		
3	Humanities	C
4	French	B or C (These are all predictions.)
3	Sociology	A or B
3	Phys. Sci.	B
1	Phy. Educ.	?
3	Pol. Sci.	D (will explain)

17 hrs.

At first I could not understand the concepts involved in political science but as the time progresses I believe I understand more about the concepts. At any rate this grade will not be recorded as well as the others since it represents only the mid-semester work. However, if I do not get a grade of "B" or better at the

The Making of a Morehouse Man

end of the semester I think I should drop the course because I want at least a "B" average in my major.

I think I will fly home. It's $23 one-way. This includes student rate and reserved seat. I am going to write Mr. Marks and inquire about a job at his store. That's all.

Love,
Spencer

Since I had a class the day after Thanksgiving, I decided it was best to remain on campus. Many other students found themselves faced with the same predicament. So, we made the best of it. Because this was my first holiday as a member of Kappa Alpha Psi, I was excited to remain in Atlanta as the fraternity's family members throughout the city opened their doors to us. I was a guest at the home of my fraternity brother Victor Wright, a native of Atlanta and a junior. His father, Mr. Lowry Wright, who died the summer before my sophomore year, had also been Kappa and was a man I had come to know during my pledge period the semester before. Our chapter would traditionally take pledge classes to the homes of Kappas, "volunteering" us for work that might be required at a brother's home. It was a wonderful opportunity to come to know older, accomplished Kappas in this way. It proved for me a great way to get to know my big brother Victor as simply a guy attending school with a real live family with which we could connect. I came to know all of the family: Vic's mother, Mrs. Pauline Wright and his two sisters Pamela and Paula. One of the great things about a work assignment at the Wright's home was that Mrs. Wright would always prepare a sumptuous luncheon that made the toil well worth it. Probably as a result of this experience, Victor became one of my closest and dearest friends.

My first Thanksgiving away from home was a time of great revelry. Victor had just acquired a new British green MGB convertible roadster that was one of the hottest car of that era and enormously popular among college students. Until this time, I had not had a great deal of experience driving. While I had learned to drive at 16, I did not have many opportunities to do so while in Atlanta. My friendship with Victor and the trust he placed in me enabled me to drive his MG. We got to know many a back road during that Thanksgiving weekend and he introduced me to Spelman women, also at home for Thanksgiving who were his friends from childhood.

5

Dec. 1, 1966

Dear Folks,

    I was just as disappointed as you that I did not get a chance to talk with you on Thanksgiving. The phone that I have access to was being used all day that day. This phone is the only one in a dormitory complex of eight dorms (the other phones were destroyed by delinquents). When I did get a chance to use it (about 4:55 CST) it would not take my dime. The personnel department was closed that day, therefore, I could not use that phone. So I became disgusted and gave up regretting it later that night.
    I will need the money and pin by Monday Dec. 5. I have not had time to look into the necessary details of getting home because pledging and school has kept me on campus pretty much but with the student rate it would be about the same as a train trip. Sometime next week I will let you know about this.

                          Love,
                          Spencer

I could have found a phone somewhere on campus from which to call home. By not doing so, however, I was again finding a way of asserting my independence from home. But as the day wore on I began to regret my decision. Thanksgiving was not just a national holiday when families got together. It was truly a spe-

Above Our Heads

cial day for my family. It was a time when I could graphically understand the value of home; the importance of family became most evident on this occasion. While I was really desirous of my freedom from parental dominance, that fabled "warm fuzzy feeling" was evoked when I was in the comfort of my grandparents' home, the perennial site for what was always a huge Thanksgiving dinner. Towards the end of that particular Thanksgiving, I was beginning to feel sorry for myself and wishing that I could have been enjoying my grandmother's excellent cooking.

But meeting women from Spelman in a more relaxed environment than the campus scene was a worthy trade-off. Anne Lanier was a sophomore who, like myself, was headed towards a major in English literature. We hit it off rather well except for one very important area of concern. She had been dating my fraternity brother Charles Cabbage who was enormously popular at Morehouse as a leading scorer, forward and captain on the basketball team. My bond with a fraternity brother would have been adequate to arrest any urge I might have entertained to pursue Anne. Yet, there was also the knowledge that Cabbage did not take kindly to interlopers. All I had to do was recall his rather firm manner while I pledged and that certainly was more than enough to carry my interests in the fairer sex elsewhere. Yet, Anne and her friends were engaging and our fun, though continuous and raucous, was respectful of relationships.

The Making of a Morehouse Man

6

Jan. 10, 1967

Dear Folks,

    Train was tremendously packed with soldiers and anyone else who could get on. Arrived in Atlanta at 10:00 AM Monday morning.
    I paid $524.00 at registration in September. My loan only covered $150-. After paying the $524 -, however, I had yet to pay $235 -. Therefore, I owe $85-. Of course this includes lab fees in French and Physical Science. This is all I owe for the semester. I believe it adds up; refer to catalogue ($750 - per semester + lab fees, books, etc.).
    I'm doing all right. 2nd semester money should be here before Jan. 28, 1967.

Love,
Spencer

Christmas of 1966 was pure happiness. I returned to Chicago as a Kappa, a Morehouse Kappa. In my mind, it seemed like things could not get any better. During the year-and-a-half that I was a student there, it seemed as though knowledge of the school was starting to spread throughout America's Black community at an astonishing rate. Where before, when I entered, few seemed to know of the college's existence, but by the end of 1966, many more apparently had come to discover her. So, upon returning to the Kappa House in Chicago on S. Ellis Avenue, I was greeted by the Kappas, the guys that I had looked up to for so many years before, now not only for the first time as a peer, but one from Morehouse. The school was slowly becoming recognized as a prominent all-men's college, not withstanding its identity as a southern Black one.

At Christmas the Kappa House always had something going on. I had been there many times before, a few times during the summer before while a Scroller. The only reason that I did not get hazed was because I was not "on line" during the summer break. But I could tell by the way those brothers looked at me that they would have relished giving a Scroller a nice little workout, since the chapter currently had no pledge class. Nevertheless, I was allowed to enjoy, in a limited capacity, the picnics and other summer events the chapter sponsored. On my first night in the House as a Brother, those same guys opened their arms to me and welcomed me fully.

"Barbara, Roxanne, Georgette, I would like you to meet our newest brother, the Pi Chapter Nupe," Robert offered. Robert Johnson, later to become CEO of Black Entertainment Network [BET], was one of the most popular members of Alpha Rho chapter.

"What's a Pi Chapter Nupe?" they excitedly asked. I was in heaven. Here were these attractive young ladies taking an interest in me because I was a Kappa. Or maybe it was because they found out that Pi Chapter was at Morehouse. Whatever the reason, for the next few hours all of my pledging memories ceased to be a source of pain. It now completely made sense. To the victor goes the spoils and I was more than ready to begin receiving mine.

When I returned to campus after the holidays, I greeted Hawes, Hense and Merritt and we all exchanged excited stories about our Christmas breaks. Because Donald Hense was from St. Louis, his experience was similar to mine in that both Chicago and St. Louis had alumni or city chapters that were more than 55 years old and with tons of brothers in both cities, each with a large fraternity house. Yet, Merritt and Hawes, though both Georgians from rural settings, had equally enriching experiences because of family and friends in their hometowns who had also pledged and returned home for the holidays.

Above Our Heads

7

Feb. 9.1967

Dear Folks,

    I understand that you are undergoing a minor financial dilemma yet you also asked if there was anything I needed. The Founders' week activities will commence on Sunday, Feb. 12, and continue through to the following Sunday. I would greatly appreciate a fairly sizable sum of money ($35, $40, etc.) to confront the situation well-prepared. If, however, you cannot do this I will understand. As you well know I am not accustomed to the habit of asking for money, therefore, I will not be let down greatly if I am without funds to share in the festivities.

    How is everyone? Are Marvin and Billy all right? Was Pepper's death confirmed? I have managed to buy my books for the courses of the second semester and supplies from the money earned from my job.

    Enclosed is receipt for 1st - 2nd semester payments. $85 - has completed payments for the first semester. The $287.50 balance from the $372.50 you sent coupled with my second semester loan of $150- came to a total of $437.50, the required amount of money due at registration. I now owe a second semester balance of $380 - as is indicated on the receipt. Everything is in order! Grades (official) will arrive either in February or March.

Love,
Spencer

The Making of a Morehouse Man

Though my tuition, room, board and all expenses only totaled $1,200 for the entire year during 1965-66, increasing only $300 per year thereafter, my brothers and I were given an early and continuing education on the value of money. When I got to Morehouse, this knowledge was not lost. I was neither among the more affluent nor the least, but my family had to make every nickel count. I had brothers who were hot on my heels on a track to college, so while my parents were sending me through, they were also trying to save for my brothers who were one year apart from each other.

I had a number of jobs while at Morehouse. From working in the dining room at Spelman to finding employment in the stacks at Trevor Arnett Library, all gave me a little spending money, precluding the need to receive an allowance from home. Yet one of my most interesting jobs was working for Dr. Melvin Dow Kennedy.

Dr. Kennedy was a no-nonsense Yankee from Massachusetts who was educated at Clark University (Worcester, MA), where he received both the A.M. and A.B. degrees and earned his Ph.D. from the University of Chicago. I had done well in his class and he had became a mentor and friend. One day he proposed that I become his assistant. One of his responsibilities, beyond his teaching duties, was to arrange for special events to be held in the chapel. He was not the coordinator of religious events but rather the one responsible for scheduling speakers who addressed the emerging issues of the day. It was here that I saw and heard, up close and personal, Stokely Carmichael, Howard Thurman, Martin Luther King, Jr. and the top federal officials of that time.

I was specifically responsible for publicizing these events Dr.

Above Our Heads

Kennedy would plan. This meant that I was to create fliers, posters or any other cheap but effective way of getting out the word. What I most liked about this assignment was that I could work on my own schedule and Dr. Kennedy trusted me to report to him how much time I actually spent working. No middle manager; just me and Dr. Kennedy.

Like so many of our professors, Dr. Kennedy would invite students to his home for an informal meal and discussion. All of our professors to a greater or lesser degree, influenced us beyond the time spent in the classroom. Yet, it was Melvin Kennedy that I remember most as assuring me that I could do all that I wanted if I simply focused on the important things: studies, studies, studies. Dr. Kennedy was heartbroken when he learned that I had pledged a fraternity. He saw the Greek life as a waste of time that added nothing to fulfilling the mission of college.

It was during these less formal occasions that we experienced learning that merged the academic with commonsense applications. It was probably the last time that I recall being told by a group leader (usually the hosting teacher), that we could be completely free to express ourselves without reprisal and it would be true. No matter what the subject, no matter how sensitive, critical or derogatory, we would not have to fear punitive actions or have confidences betrayed. Since that time, whenever I have been offered these assurances, especially in a job-related context, they have never been honored.

8

Feb. 20, 1967

Dear Folks,

    I have received the money and had a most enjoyable weekend. Thank Mrs. Hambright for me I appreciated the five dollars very much. I met Dr. Lane and he was kind enough to purchase me a Centennial Banquet ticket along with the other fellows from Chicago. The alumni returned in droves. It was quite a festive occasion.

    I have moved to a new location - Bennet Hall. The price change is extremely nominal (check catalogue) but it is well worth it. I now have a closet, dresser, desk, bookshelves, bed that are all my own. With the exception of a bed, I had none of these in Unit 1 Rm. 201. My new address is Bennet Hall, 645 Beckwith St., S.W. I also have a new mailbox which is located at this dormitory. It is #302. My room number is #301 and my roommate who is an Alpha is Sam Wilder. That's another good thing, I now only have one other roommate where as before I had three other roommates.

    Granddaddy might be interested to know that I met a Dr. More (or Moore) who practices dentistry in Chicago, (is a Kappa) and knows Grandmother and him quite well. The guest speaker for a number of ceremonies was Howard Thurman '23. He is a Morehouse grad (note the numbers following his name) and author of seventeen books (I don't know the name of one!).

Above Our Heads

Cindy and I are still with each other. I bought her some Valentine candy. She appreciated it tremendously. I feel terrible that I neglected you the way I did, Mom. I will make up for it some way.

What are weather conditions like? What did you hear from House of Vision about those glasses I ordered. I could use them now since I recently broke a lens on the glasses I now have. I have, however, been wearing those industrial glasses but because they are heavier than a normal pair of glasses I don't wear them as often as I should. Yet, if you are not able to pick them up or they no longer have them then I will continue to wear the safety glasses until I am able to purchase some myself.

How is Marvin & Billy? They doing all right in school? Did you get Marvin those shoes? Bye for now.

Love,
Spencer

The most important school event after homecoming was the annual Founder's Day celebration. In 1967, Morehouse was 100 years old and I was fortunate enough to be a student there at that time. Being from Chicago probably gave me a leg up in the eyes of one of the college's largest alumni donors. Dr. Alvin Hubert Lane, a member of the Class of 1919, was practicing dentistry in Chicago and knew my grandfather, Dr. William C. Gibbs, also a practicing dentist in Chicago. Because Dr. Lane was a member of the college's board of trustees and therefore, intimately involved with and concerned about Morehouse, he was a welcomed presence to the events marking the centennial year of the college.

The Making of a Morehouse Man

Like all Morehouse social gatherings, heavily attended by alumni, there was always great merrymaking. It was at these occasions where a Morehouse student could drink liquor, if they wished, as long as they at least acted as if they knew what they were doing. While drinking on campus was officially prohibited, it frequently did occur by the overwhelming majority of students. Though the rum-and-coke was clearly the most popular drink at football games, dinners and receptions always seem to be the occasion where you would hear "scotch-and-soda" being ordered or maybe the occasional "scotch-on-the-rocks," but never did I ever see anyone drinking "scotch neat." It became clearer and clearer to all of us in the younger classes that scotch drinks were considered a drink of status. Experience soon taught us that it was a drink for which one had to develop a taste, unlike the Coca-cola-sweetened rum drink. Yet, even those who presumed to name scotch their drink had not developed so great a taste for it that they were ordering it "neat," that is, without ice. Yet, when those of us less experienced drinkers wanted to impress the alumni at such occasions, we would order scotch and appear to enjoy it as much as those whom we aspired to be.

Bennet Hall was the residence for juniors and seniors. So, when I, a second semester sophomore, was allowed to transfer there, I thought of myself as somehow greatly privileged and to this day, have no idea how I was fortunate enough to land there. Bennet Hall was the farthest Morehouse outpost from the main campus, but was still nestled within the larger campus community of the Atlanta University Center (AUC, as it had come to be called). Actually, Bennet was physically on the campus of the Interdenominational Theological Center, the AUC's consortium of divinity schools. Bennet Hall, while a property of the college, contained the administrative offices of the Morehouse School of Religion, a graduate institution, long ago made independent of the college. It also housed the Morehouse seminarians at ITC. As a sophomore, I was among the youngest students then living in Bennet Hall. This fact had an enormous impact on the maturation process. While these were all still students, they were persons who had variously walked pass the threshold of boyhood into manhood. The seminarians really caused the average age of residents to rise since many of these men were married and returned home to families and pulpits on the weekend. Bennet was a serious place that promoted thoughtfulness and order that the other residential buildings either could not do or chose not to do. Because Bennet Hall had just been dedicated in April, 1965, and was therefore the newest, most modern hall, there was tremendous pride in it that had a great deal to do with why it was scrupulously maintained and life within it was more controlled than in other places. I had lived in residences on campus before where frustrated students, primarily freshmen, perhaps the occasional sophomore, would shove an angry fist through a wall, leaving a gaping hole in the wall. This would never have been tolerated in Bennet and if defacement of property were ever to occur, it would be addressed by removal of that student from the dormitory or worse.

One of the most delightful events for me was meeting my roommate Samuel G. Wilder, Jr. Sam, from Rome, Georgia, was a member of a prominent family that distinguished itself in the funeral service business. He was one of the few students able to possess a car on campus, even though Bennet Hall students had a

The Making of a Morehouse Man

higher number of students owning and having cars than other members of the student body. It was not just any car either. Sam had a 1966 Dodge Charger, which was the hottest of the "muscle cars" of that day. Another student and "homeboy" of Sam's from Rome, John Houser, also had one of these cars. Along with Carl Bowman from Memphis, who lived across the hall from Sam and me, I had found myself in a completely different company of friends.

Sam, John and Carl were all juniors; therefore, while I was accepted into their company, I was suspect largely because I was the new kid on the block and they had all been together for two-and-a-half years by the time they had come to meet me. Yet, they were not such an exclusive "clique" that I would not eventually become fully accepted. While Sam and John were on a track toward medical careers, Carl was an aspiring businessman. Sam was a member of Alpha Phi Alpha and John was Phi Beta Sigma. Carl was a member of the only Greek-letter fraternity unique to Morehouse at that time, Phi Lambda.

One of the other very important advantages of living with a guy who owned a car was that if one of us got hungry, we could always pile into Sam's car and head for huge hamburgers. While my fraternity friendships afforded the same privilege, it was the immediate availability and willingness of Sam to instigate or accommodate the urge to undertake a "food run." The first time that I had ever heard anyone suggesting that we all go and get a Whopper, I had no idea what was being talked about. I thought it was an invitation to engage in some shady activity. One of the fast food chains, which were beginning to pop up in Atlanta, had recently introduced this sandwich, the Whopper, and somehow I had completely missed hearing about it.

It was immensely satisfying to encounter one new experience after the other which these upperclassmen were so willing to share with me in their journeys of growth and development. I was especially happy to learn that solid relationships with my schoolmates did not end with the alliances formed in my freshman year nor with my fraternity brothers. There were a great many wonderful fellows throughout the community of Morehouse.

The Making of a Morehouse Man

9

April 19, 1967

Dear Folks,

Honestly I wasn't aware of how quickly time was passing and how my letters had temporarily come to an abrupt stop. Accept my apologies.

Of course, certainly, without doubt, I will enthusiastically work with (or for) Mr. Bell and the CYO. Why I have already forgotten about the beautiful country Portland, Oregon has to offer.

I arrived in Atlanta at 12:00pm (noon). Still, however, I was delayed three (3) hours and my sentiments on that ride are the same as those on the ride prior to it - TERRIBLE. I'm thoroughly convinced that trains are the most uncomfortable, time-consuming, inconvenient form of transportation offered . Unless, however, one travels by Pullman. At least one can sleep on a facsimile of a bed and is not annoyed by the other restless passengers.

There is now an organized CONSCIENTIOUS OBJECTOR program active on the Morehouse campus. I don't guarantee a riot-free area but I don't believe that a development similar to the Fisk breakout shall occur.

School always has had and, I have resolved, always will have its drawbacks, yet I am not doing too badly this semester. My Writing of Poetry class is a joy to me and I am making great strides in the area of writing poetry. I am now compiling a collection of poems which are designed to reflect my innerself. So far it has received enthusiastic support from my instructor and

Above Our Heads

has provided meaning in the deepest sense for me.
How are Marvin and Billy?
I will be coming home! That's all for now.

         Love,
         Spencer

My feelings then about train travel vacillated according to the experience of the most immediate ride. Still, the air travel industry was so aggressive in wooing student passengers, that if you wanted to be some place "yesterday," then flying was the hands-down choice. And when the train ride was packed with students heading home, nothing was more fun. The Louisville & Nashville ran between Chicago and Atlanta and stopped at significant points in between. While not many Spelman women boarded the train home, instead choosing the plane or Daddy's invitation to be picked up from school, there was one group who boarded that were always excitedly anticipated.

 The L&N stopped in Nashville, Tennessee and to our great delight the women from Fisk heading north preferred, it seemed, rail travel. For whatever reasons, Fisk seemed to attract a more geographically diverse student body. Spelman at the time was like Morehouse, a regional rather than national school. Fisk, on the other hand, drew the nation to its campus. So while there were very few Spelmanites en route to Chicago, there were huge numbers of Fisk women returning home. My Aunt Grace had graduated from there a few years earlier, meeting and marrying a Meharry dentist along the way.

 While the first term did not end at Morehouse until after

The Making of a Morehouse Man

examinations following the Christmas break, Fisk students had completed their first semester's studies before Christmas. Upon boarding the train, they were ready to party. In a way, it was a good thing that Spelman women did not make this trip. It gave those of us from Atlanta an opportunity to know our "cousins" from Nashville.

One of the features of life aboard the train that I found particularly enjoyable was that, once again, if you wore a suit and tie you were treated like an adult. So the appropriately attired always converged upon the barcar and were given service just as any adult would expect to receive. In both Illinois and Georgia, in order to legally purchase liquor, one had to be 21. On the rails, "carding," if ever required, was never done.

Because we were returning home to the best holiday season of the year, there was a lot to anticipate with our new friends from Nashville. If one were a fraternity man, all the better. The Kappa House would be alive and well throughout the Christmas season and most Chicago college students, men and women, wanted to party with Kappas. I could easily score extra points by not only announcing my fraternal affiliation, but also by inviting young coeds to the Kappa House. By the time the L&N pulled into Union Station, budding romances might be underway. We would always see the women that we met at parties throughout the holidays.

Of course the Vietnam War was a growing concern throughout the nation and especially among college students. And, nowhere was it more true than at Morehouse where the student body was exclusively young, male and Black. Some of my schoolmates, especially those from the South where there seemed to be a greater interest in military service, left school voluntarily to join the armed forces. Many of these students were either in academic trouble or growing bored and saw this as a way to do something more constructive with their lives. Most of us, however, were protesting the war and/or doing all that we could to insure that we would not be drafted.

Suddenly, we all became astute students of African American male history. We knew full well that our male ancestors who fought in previous wars came back to a nation that they defended only to return to the racism which they left. Brothers at Morehouse knew that this country has never cared for the welfare of Black men more than when we were property. Then, we were valued as goods. Our worth lay not in our humanity but in the value of our utility. And just as in those times of slavery, Black men were still being sold if a profit could be realized. This time the buyer was the military-industrial complex that needed foot soldiers. I believe that Morehouse men saw in Vietnam not only an unjust war to those whom we were fighting but it was a continuing injustice to those who looked upon it as the only means by which they could be employed and therefore defined. If you graduated from high school with no prospects for further formal education, then the military was believed to be a viable option. Yet, for these men, service in the military would not be the extra-added credential needed to assure political success once deciding to enter a life of politics upon discharge. One still needed college. It made no difference if you served valiantly. We soon learned that America itself lost respect for the war, and so for the longest time following its end, Vietnam veterans were regarded in the most unfavorable light. There was no way that most of us were

The Making of a Morehouse Man

willing to go to this war voluntarily.

When the conscientious objector movement landed at Morehouse, it was for the most part welcomed. Any legitimate means of avoiding Vietnam was seen as far superior to going to war. This included protest marches and rallies, even when they resulted in arrest. It was during this time that Malcolm X and Martin Luther King, Jr., neither of whom early on had been publically vocal on the issue of Vietnam, began criticizing the war. This was all it took for Morehouse to rally around the anti-war efforts.

Many students began to emerge as leaders in the peace movement on Morehouse's campus and throughout the AUC. There was Harvey Smith, an Atlantan member of my class and the son of a dentist who had graduated from Morehouse in the '40s. He became a Muslim while in school and a vitriolic, if not highly effective, speaker on the injustices facing Black America, generally and the negative implications of our participation in Vietnam, specifically. There were many others who took to a public podium to express what was an increasing outrage at the war that seemed to threaten the future of Black America by siphoning off Black male leadership. While there was a growing number of competent public speakers developing, protest was also becoming evident in the arts and literature.

10

May 3, 1967

Dear Folks,
 As always I appreciated the money you sent. Everything is fine here. I am acting editor of the campus literary magazine THE NEW CATALYST. The article you sent was quite interesting as I was able to read it with an open mind. It was, however, quite in opposition to the views of the school populace. Too pro-American!
 Has Granddaddy repaired his offices yet? I imagine he has by now, but...
 It should be interesting to see the decoration of 16139 So. Wolcott. I can hardly wait. How is neighborhood vice? Still on the rampage?
 That tornado was quite devastating as was indicated by the reports received in Atlanta. You were fortunate living in Markham. Relieved to hear no harm came to Grandmother and Granddaddy and the Finchs. Is everyone doing okay? I would love to fly home. I will get out of school about the same time as last year (around May 31-June 1). I need some funds:
 a) $20- I have been appointed a delegate from my fraternity to attend the Southeast Provincial meeting from all Kappa chapters in Ga., South Carolina, North Carolina). This will pay for lodging. Fraternity will pay registration fee for conference and transportation. (Send before May 10th). Held in Columbus, Georgia.
 b) $8.50 Every year Pi Chapter (Morehouse) gives what is called the Kappa Dawn Dance.

The Making of a Morehouse Man

Will be the morning (2am to 6am) before graduation (May 29th, I believe). This is the price each brother has to pay in order to make dance possible (expenses of band, location, etc.). Need this before May 15th. This is usually an extremely successful affair. That's all.

Love,
Spencer

I had become involved in the campus literary magazine as acting editor. Within a very short time I would become editor-in-chief. Entitled *The New Catalyst,* it was published twice a year, once each semester. In the spring of 1967, that particular issue won a second place award from the Washington-based Committee on College Literary Magazines. A section of this issue was devoted to thoughts about the Vietnam War. Students everywhere were becoming increasingly outspoken about wanting to see an end to what was believed to be an unjust war. These poems, which ranged from sonnets to free verse to haiku, largely addressed Morehouse's discontentment with the U.S. presence in Vietnam. Here are three submissions from that issue of *The New Catalyst:*

ASIAN STEW

Wit rice-n-mud-n-bamboo shoots
Wit sizzled hairs-n-human eclairs
Wit shrapnel-n-goodwill-n-jelly
Jelly jelly

-Bob Terrell

Above Our Heads

G. I. HIGH

G. I. Boots
  for sale
    in an
    old
               funky shop   Two slant-eyed
women
      selling it
      for about
      a dollar
Bought some
  it was good
    Get some
      later
Got to fight V. C.   A red-light district
        Full of hoods and gangs
          And vice
      two hip cats high on shit
      Walking cool, smoking a joint
      shot down in the streets
      by two ambulance drivers
    Sitting down
      digging a
      sound
    Dylan or Miles
      it don't matter
      High
    the sound
      my mind
        blank

        -Warren Hewitt

The Making of a Morehouse Man

And then there were poems that expressed our disdain for having to fight a war abroad, while many of our people had to live in dehumanizing conditions at home:

UNTITLED

the old gray-haired black woman
out in dusty cotton field
heat from sun burning skin
aching back bent, hoe in hands
killing cotton plants like machine
hating, sweating, hating, sweating
ten hour, end of day
fru'm white man three hours pay
riding through town on back of truck
in stinking torn up work clothes
must get off in town
walking to ten cent store
white people pass raising noses

   In ten cent store
young white girl shouting
   "What you want?"
50 cent envelopes, 25 cent paper, 30 cent stamps
money to young white girl
walking home package in hand
two miles dusty road
young white boys passing in speeding car
home, old ugly sagging wood house
chickens in yard
children playing soldier with sticks
up rotten stairs
across creeking porch
into dark house, opening package

Above Our Heads

> writing
>> Dear Son,
>>> we misses you so. we
>> needs you here to help us but
>> you had to go.
>>> How is things over there?
>>> You be sho and
>> keep your pretty uniform
>> all cleaned up...
>>>> -Milton James

When word had circulated that *The New Catalyst* had won a national award for its prior issue, upperclassmen began taking the publication more seriously. In subsequent issues, many Spelman students submitted work. As a result of the award and growing interest among the many students in our world, we helped in a small way to put Morehouse on the collegiate literary map. Much more exciting to me than this was having been elected a chapter delegate to the southeast province meeting of Kappa Alpha Psi to be held in Columbus, Georgia that spring.

James Hawes and I had been very close during our pledge period. Our devotion to Kappa was clearly obvious. We enjoyed each other's company tremendously, so when we were asked by our brothers to represent the chapter at this meeting, it was our great honor and privilege to attend. We knew, too, that we were going to have an enormously good time. Neophytes were always loved by the chapter that initiated them as well as by other brothers who would learn of their status. A Neophyte was one who was a member of the most recent group of intiates. Once a new group of Scrollers was brought on board and subsequently initiated, the

The Making of a Morehouse Man

Neophytes lost that status and it passed to the newer group of Kappas. Neophytes brought the type of joy to a chapter that a newborn baby brings to a family. Everyone gathers around to protect, care and nurture these new brothers into the meaning of fraternity. I did not think that this would be distinguishable from the feelings that we had as Morehouse men, as we were already part of a corps of Black men absorbing the school's well-known traditions and participating in its time-tested mission. Yet fraternity life was different.

When we got to Columbus, we checked into our rooms and immediately were invited to a reception to meet other brothers from the region. Thinking that we would dazzle our small-town brothers with our big-city sophistication, we sauntered into the large room where registration was taking place, then stopped, stunned. Even in Atlanta, we had not experienced the fraternity in as lavish a setting as there in Columbus that evening.

The older brothers in the fraternity knew how to put young upstarts in their place. A few of them began to remark that they were happy that neophytes were present because now they would be able to complete their initiation process. WE THOUGHT-NO! WE KNEW THAT WE HAD UNDERGONE ALL OF THE RIGHTS OF INITIATION INTO THE FRATERNITY!!! WHAT ON EARTH COULD THESE GUYS BEING TALKING ABOUT!!! Hawes and I looked at each other as if to say to the other that maybe coming here was not such a good idea after all. We began to think that our brothers back at school had set us up and that we were in for more humiliation or worse. Other brothers, seeing our obvious distress, cracked up uncontrollably. Upon regaining their composure, they walked towards us, extending their hands in friendship, assuring us that neophytes always are the butt of "initiation jokes" because the response was always so predictable. When Hawes and I talked about it later, we admitted to each other that we were looking for a way of discreetly leaving the room before whatever initiation was planned occurred.

It was a wonderful evening. The brothers of the host chapter rolled out the royal carpet, letting out all the stops. The buffet table was ladened with steaks, chops, seafood, cooked in the wonderful southern style that I had come to love. That evening, Hawes and I experienced our first full bar with white-jacketed waiters who would serve us whatever we wanted without charge to us. We thanked our lucky stars for pledging Kappa. And then, just when we thought that things could not improve, a door was opened and in walked the female friends of the members of the fraternity

Of course, there were present the wives and girlfriends of the local brothers present. Yet these guys were thoughtful enough to invite a number of very personable women to join us on our first night. This is when I saw that when one works hard towards a goal and achieves it, the rewards extend far beyond the sought-after goal. All I had wanted to accomplish was to become a part of the fraternity to make my life on campus more enjoyable. I had no idea that the bonds that held my chapter brothers in community with one another were just as profoundly evident throughout the entire fraternity.

That weekend, I met a number of Kappas who were alumni of Morehouse and who had settled in Columbus and the surrounding area. These men especially greeted Hawes and me

The Making of a Morehouse Man

warmly because of our shared experience of Morehouse. With the other Kappas who were present, we learned much more about the traditions of Kappa, while becoming acquainted with those from Pi who could be helpful to us as we neared graduation. And while all of the men present were Kappas, those of us who had been initiated at Morehouse, whether 30 years ago or last week, felt that school tie binding us all the more closely together. It is difficult to describe what I believed to be a spiritual force linking us to one another. In all honesty, even today, I feel a heightened sense of camaraderie when in the company of Morehouse men that does not exist for me within the other professional and fraternal circles in which I am privileged to hold membership.

Above Our Heads

The Making of a Morehouse Man

YEAR THREE

This splendid school for men, this pleasant place,
This home of wisdom, this abode of truth,
This other Athens, shrine of Academe,
This mecca, planned by Freedom for her use
Against oppression and the threat of force;
This noble tribe of youth, this mighty band,
This shining beacon on a Georgia hill,
Which keeps before mankind such lofty aims
And lights the pathway to a better world
Against the social ills that cause decay;
This favored seat, this place, this school, this Morehouse,
This Alma Mater of a noble breed
Known for their faith and honored for their truth,
Far-famed for courage and for manly deeds,
For deep devotion to God and state,
For Christian service to their fellow men,
For firm commitment to democracy;
This school of such rare souls, this dear, dear school
Known for her worthy sons throughout the world.

Anonymous, published on the
Cover of the Morehouse College
Catalogue, 1969-70.

1

Sept. 28, 1967

Dear Folks,

I realize nothing I can say will excuse my writing so late. I arrived in Atlanta at approx. 5:00 EST. I left O'Hara at 2:45 CST.

I am living in Rm 117 Mays Hall. My box number is 299. The address should be written:

> S.C. Gibbs
> Box 299
> Morehouse College
> Atlanta, Georgia

My courses are:

Intro. To Shakespeare	3hrs.
Neo-Classical Writers	3hrs
Public Speaking	3hrs.
Survey of English Literature	3hrs.
Religion	3hrs.
Piano I*	2hrs

*The piano course is one in the actual teaching of how to play rather than theory. Because of a familiarity with music I received in high school I believe I should learn quite rapidly.

I am working at the Spelman College Dining Hall making $15.00 per week plus meals. Because you paid the full 606.50 at registration time I received 60.00 as refund for turning in my meal book (relinquishing

The Making of a Morehouse Man

"board" privileges at Morehouse).
The job has nothing but advantages:
1) Eat as much as you want and what you want.
2) Save $45 on each $81 payment (three more, remember?). Therefore, send only $36.00 per payment.
3) Because its necessary to get up early (for the breakfast meal) one does not easily miss
his classes esp. if they are at 8:00AM (my Neo-Classical writers course).
4) $15.00 per week (therefore do not send any allowance).
By the way $30- of the $60- I got back went towards the purchase of glasses and the remaining $30- in my bank account (savings) down here.
All of my books have been purchased with the exception of a few which I can easily take care of.
I got the grade from Spelman put on my record at Morehouse. If I can catch up with the coach I'll get my "Inc." in P.E. changed probably to an "A" or "B."

Love,
Spencer

I was entering my third year of school and was assigned to Mays Hall, the on-campus dormitory for junior and senior students. Although it was considered prestigious to live in Mays, it was now used by sophomores as well. After Bennett Hall the previous semester, this felt like a step backwards. However, it was close to classrooms and it was the dormitory closest to Spelman. My roommate was a congenial fellow from South Orange, New Jersey named Edgar Thomas, whose father was a Baptist pastor in that town.

Above Our Heads

Edgar was to be my seventh roommate in five semesters. I understand that there were guys who had the same roommate for their entire four years. This was not to be the case with me nor was it to be true for the overwhelming majority of us. I began to like the "newness" that was created by each semester. Except for my freshman year, I had not lived in the same place for two consecutive semesters.

Edgar was a track man, a cross-country runner and a bit of a bohemian type. He always wore sunglasses, inside and out. At first I thought it was partly affectation, but as I got to know him, he proved to be a genuine down-to-earth guy. Even though we were both juniors, I had not known Edgar before rooming with him. He transferred to Morehouse some time during our sophomore year and though I may have seen him from afar, our paths would not have had occasion to naturally cross. Though the school was small, with less than a total population of 1,000, you
may still not come to know all of the other members of your class beyond their names. Because of this, moving each semester caused me to mix with a wide variety of people that living in one place with the same roommate could not allow. Somehow, I was able to shrug off the feelings that it was either something I said or did that found me moving each semester.

Around this time, my friends and I had discovered a beer store very near the Spelman Yard, as her campus was called, that sold tap beer in half gallon Mason or Ball jars. For $1.50, one could get a large jar of beer and have a party in your room or picnic on one of the various stretches of lawn that covered points between Spelman and Morehouse very easily, but with only the highest amount of discretion. In all the time we had these beer soirees, no one ever

The Making of a Morehouse Man

broke one of those cumbersome and often slippery jars. The reason was simple: the store owner charged $2.00 for the jar which you could use again and again. Of course, if you went for beer without the refillable jar, you'd have to pay the guy another $2.00 plus the $1.50 to fill it. This was just not going to happen to any self-respecting Morehouse man. As one can see, the jar was more valuable than the beer it would hold and, therefore, many alliances would be made for an evening between one who owned a jar and another who had $1.50.

I cannot state with any degree of certainty, but I sometimes wondered if my friends and I were not becoming a bad influence upon Edgar. When we started bringing these large quantities of beer to the room, sometimes as many as two or three of these half-gallon jars, Edgar was there to enjoy it along with the rest of us, always offering to contribute financially his fair share. Because he was an athlete and the son of a minister, I wondered aloud one day if he was all right with our activity. Said Edgar, "my Father has a special mission as a minister and I have my duties as a student. I respect his and he respects mine." That ended my concerns.

During this semester, I had a job in the Spelman dining hall. One of my roommates from the first semester of my sophomore year, Larry Burt, helped me to get it and was a co-worker. Every day, for all three meals, we would go to the kitchen at Spelman, receive as much food as we wanted, and wash the dishes afterwards. While we were not allowed to eat with the women, we could often converse with them as they disposed of their dishes. We were, after all, students just as they were, so the school was not terribly rigid about discouraging fraternization with Morehouse students. And we were still youngsters, Larry at 20 and a senior and me 19 years

Above Our Heads

old. We were from time to time prone to show-off. One day we were holding this informal contest to see how many dish trays we could carry to replace the ones students would receive at the beginning of the cafeteria line. Once a tray was returned by an individual student upon completion of a meal, it and the dishes it held would be cleaned and stacked for the next group of students who may enter or the next day's meal. The clean stack had to be carried from the kitchen to the start of the serving line. While this was not a terribly long distance, the walk placed you in full view of anyone seated in the dining area.

The contest was going fine, each one of us carrying a larger and larger stack. What made this all the more delightfully absurd was that the women would cheer us on, encouraging us to increase our load even more with each carry. When I made what was to be my last attempt, just as I reached the point where I was to set the trays down, I dropped them. It made such a huge commotion that the kitchen staff rushed into the dining area, not knowing what had happened. Instructors and other college personnel, previously riveted to their seats, were wrenched from their meals. But the students gave the most demonstrative reaction. Their laughter could have raised the roof on a less substantial building. There was nowhere to hide. I felt five inches tall and my cheeks were burning with embarrassment. Even Larry, my buddy, co-worker and fellow contestant joined in the laughter that had everyone in stitches. To make matters worse, I had to pick up from the floor what must have been close to seventy trays, all the while the object of all of their humiliating cackling. I swore I would never intentionally place myself in a situation where I could possibly become the object of ridicule again and to insure it, I

The Making of a Morehouse Man

vowed that I would quit as soon as I could return to the kitchen, bringing to it trays that now had to be re-washed.

Interestingly, two of the students, obviously taking mercy upon my predicament, helped me collect the trays. Even the woman I had been dating at the time, someone I was sure was mortified with embarrassment, helped me. In so many words, she suggested that in the grand scheme of things, what had happened was no big thing. She added that it gave a kind of comic relief to the humdrum goings-on in the cafeteria line. As I carried the trays back, people started to applaud. Very soon I was beginning not to feel so badly about this. Later I was to be told that it took guts to hang in there and finish the job in the light of how embarrassing this must have been personally to me. At the time, however, no one could have convinced me of this.

By the next morning the entire Spelman student body had learned what happened in the dining hall the evening before. Of course there was giggling and teasing, but it seemed to be motivated more by admiration of these "kitchen helpers" from Morehouse who would dare to upset the typically staid decorum of Chivers Dining Room. During the summer following my third year, this dining hall tragically burned down. I could not help but wonder if some of our craziness did not contribute to lighting the spark.

One of the benefits of attending school in the AUC was that you could cross-register, i.e., take courses toward fulfilling your degree requirements in one of the other undergraduate colleges. It was not until many years later that a Morehouse student could take courses at Georgia Tech or elsewhere in Atlanta when courses were not available at Morehouse. At this time, even though a course may have been available from the Morehouse catalogue, one might prefer instead to register for the same course in what may have been believed to be an easier school within the AUC. For political reasons a student would never register for a course in his major at another school for fear of disappointing the chairman of the department. All courses in the major had to be taken at Morehouse unless it was over-subscribed (rarely), or needed for graduation and could not be taken in time for the graduating senior to receive his degree on time (never). The rationale for this was simple: if you came to get a Morehouse degree, then the major area of study which you elected would be comprised of courses taught by Morehouse faculty. However, a student would be allowed to take courses in excess of the requirements for the major in any school within the Center. Often a student would have to take that course in summer school, if it was offered, or wait until the following semester. This is the reason why students would sometimes take longer than four years to graduate. Poor course planning or believing that one could find a loophole disappointed and upset many a student and family from sharing in the most important day of that man's life.

Yet, in order to amass the requisite number of hours to graduate, having satisfied all requirements for the major and minor at Morehouse, a student could continue the matriculation process at Atlanta University (in special graduate areas), Clark, Morris Brown or Spelman. Most students, if they could, would try to register for something at Morris Brown because it was thought to be the easiest of the campuses to get an "A." Often this reasoning would backfire: believing it to be true, a student would not work as hard and get a lower grade. Yet, interestingly enough, students would rationalize that while the grade was less than the expected "A," they did-

The Making of a Morehouse Man

n't have to work hard to get it. Therefore, they had more time to pursue their own frivolities.

This business of "pursuing frivolities" made arriving at the decision to take a course at Spelman extremely vexing. For the most part Morehouse men saw Spelman Yard as a playground. Spelman was not thought to be a place to get an easy "A." Yet, no matter how one looked at it, it had to be more fun than sitting in a classroom of all men. The thinking went something like this: if we took courses there, would we be kidding ourselves about the work needed to finish the course with a respectable grade or were we simply that desperate to get next to these women? Most of us opted to go elsewhere, choosing to separate work from play.

Yet not wanting to decide upon too important a matter without first having a thorough investigation of the empirical evidence, I enrolled in a Spelman course. I was thoroughly distracted, vaguely recalling that it had something to do with the religious world's influence upon art. Incidentally, I was the only male student, so whenever I would be called upon to offer an opinion, I would be given a great deal of scrutiny by the other students. A discussion focusing on my often ill-informed views would go on and on to the point of personal discomfort. It was me against the 20 of them, or so it seemed. Unfortunately, I quickly began to take neither the subject matter nor the male instructor, a well-respected pastor and art historian, very seriously. What could have in fact resulted in a high grade, turned out to be something less. Now I understood why Morehouse and Spelman rarely met in the classroom.

2

Nov. 3, 1967

Dear Folks,

    I'm doing fine! If I have not expressed my thanks for the money you sent I hope you will accept it now. I'm trying to do so much that I actually don't have time to sit down and write letters. This is the third letter that I have written all year (one other to you and one to Andrea).

    I must be a manic-depressive or something like it. Some days I'm very happy and then become very depressed and for no real apparent reason. I won't go on talking about this because I do not really understand the situation. At least I believe I'm stable.

    How was your operation, Mom? I know that you told me in your last letter that everything was all right, are you still doing well?

    I still intend to go to Law School. Political Science is my minor and English is my major. I will be taking the LSAT (Law School Aptitude Test) Nov. 11. This is an eight hour examination. It will be a trial run as I am not a senior and consequently do not have to send scores to law schools yet.

    How are Marv and Billy? Is school fairing well for both of them? Enclosed is my application for renewal of my operator's license. Pay it for me and I will reimburse you (or just keep back $5.00 that you may intend to send in the future).

                                    Love,
                                      Spencer

The Making of a Morehouse Man

From the day that a student enters college, I suspect that he or she begins to think about what one wants to do with one's life. This was certainly true at Morehouse. Yet, except for those rare individuals, a freshman did not dwell too long in thinking about vocation. It was the handful of students who knew exactly what they wanted to be in life who dove in with a clear agenda from the outset. These were generally the sons of professional men who were preparing to take over Dad's practice. As for the rest of us, we did not take the calling that was to be our destiny, our life's work, too seriously until the junior year.

I believe that one of the factors that contributed to this was the conversations that the juniors were beginning to have with the seniors. For the seniors, the future was now. They were feverishly engaged in the process of applying to graduate schools, taking graduate, medical and law school admission exams. A few were even considering entering the job market immediately upon graduation. What animated these conversations most in the early stages, prior to gaining acceptance letters, was the grave concern about the entrance examinations to graduate and professional school. Many seniors who had established wonderful academic records could not fathom why they had attained scores lower than needed for entry to the schools of their choice. They experienced outright terror when their results returned with scores below what they felt would gain them unopposed entry.

Generally, freshmen and sophomores were not regarded as colleagues able to understand a senior's circumstances and the stress that person was feeling. Whether true or not, seniors did not believe that the guys in the lower classes cared or understood the gravity of their concerns. Typically, they would commiserate with one another or juniors, those they had known for the last two-and-a-half years, who might better enable them to make sense of this new phase of undergraduate life.

I can recall my own surprise and shock when some of those unarguably brilliant students shared with me their LSAT or Graduate Record Examination scores. We would quickly agree that they would take the exam a second time and take an examination preparation course to help bolster scores. When they began telling us of their regret at not having taken the preliminary exams offered to juniors, many of us immediately signed up to take them. While practice does not always make perfect, it can improve the scores on standardized tests measurably.

Morehouse had not been known as a sports powerhouse in the 1960s. As evidence of this, in the 1966-67 basketball season, her won-lost-tied record was 9-13-0. In football, for the same year, it was even more dismal: 0-8-0. Through the remainder of the '60s, those teams did not improve by huge leaps and bounds (the best W-L-T for Basketball was 8-5-0 in 69-70; for Football, 3-3-2). But the students were always supportive of its teams, win or lose. And then in the mid-'60s, the chairman of the department of physical education and coach of swimming, Dr. James "Pinky" E. Haines, began to recruit new talent for the swimming team.

Dr. Haines held a Doctor of Physical Education (D.P. Ed.) degree from Springfield College in Massachusetts and was a true visionary. He looked all the way to New York City and found some of the most incredible swimmers the South had ever seen. In the 1966-67 season, the Tigersharks had a 13-0 record, becoming first place winners in the Southeastern Intercollegiate Athletic Conference (SIAC) as well as throughout the region. This position lasted well into the Seventies.

During this period, predominately Black colleges did not compete with white schools in sporting events. Somehow, Coach Haines was able to convince the white regional officials of the NCAA and coaches of those schools that the time had come to allow interracial competition, at least in the sport of swimming. The Tigersharks became a phenomenal force with which to reckon. They handily disposed of the myth that Black men could not swim competitively against whites, beating Georgia Tech and Emory University, the two best swimming teams, until that time, in the conference.

Those first New York swimmers drafted by Coach Haines helped tremendously, along with the other team members, to turn the Tigersharks into the winningest team in Morehouse history. Richard Allen '69, Sidney Brooks '69, and Juan Lieba '69, were the first to arrive in 1965. They were followed the next year by Wigberto Cintron '70, Michael Clark '70, Michael T. Davis '70, Robert Garcia '70, and Joseph Ruscito '70 (the only one not from New York). Joining this group were Lewis Collier '71, from Buffalo, New York and Charles "Sunshine" McKenntee '71, from New York City.

In the 1965-66 season, those swimmers who were members of the Class of 1969 became campus heroes after the first competition. During that record-breaking period they were teamed with Clarence Grisham '69, Isaiah B. King '68, Howard V. Gary '68, Lambert Greene '68, Elias Burton '68, John T. Franks '69, and James Fannin, '70.

One of the interesting byproducts of swimmers from the northeast was a new kind of diversity. During the last half of the

Above Our Heads

Sixties, Morehouse was becoming more and more geographically diverse as its reputation grew and was publicized. Because a large number of the swim team now consisted of persons of Latino origin, Morehouse was beginning to become culturally diverse. It was largely these brothers, along with African-Americans from New York, who introduced Morehouse to Latin music.

While most of us were clueless regarding the popularity of salsa, most New Yorkers, as well as persons from other major cities in the northeast, were fully aware of the hot New York Latin music scene originated by the Puerto Rican-born musicians who were the purveyors of the sound. Salsa was imported to this country in the 1960s and landed in the welcoming arms of NuYoricans, as Puerto Rican immigrants living in New York City were being called. But the music took off and caught on with everyone who loved lively dance music. It was at Morehouse that I first heard the recordings of Joe Cuba, Tito Puente, The Fania All-Stars, Sonny Bravo, Joe Bataan and Charlie Palmieri. "Bang, Bang" was the most popular record heard at parties as evidenced by the fact that the host might have two copies for fear that one might get scratched or stolen.

The influence of Coach Haines' early recruitment efforts cannot be underestimated. The whole world was quickly becoming a village and Morehouse, like many places then and even now, was holding on, though not too tenaciously, to a time when Southerners defined what the college was. Those of us who were students then witnessed the passing of the old into the new and it was startling at times.

With Stokely Carmichael-led rallies focusing upon changing the unjust status of Black people and new music reflecting still

The Making of a Morehouse Man

more change, came the emergence of the use of marijuana. Pot smoking prior to 1965 was non-existent at Morehouse. If enjoyed at all, it was by a subterranean few, way off-campus, in a corner in the dark. With a changing student demography, this was to change. At first there was a sense that "users" were akin to or were criminals. Then, as time went on, people began to see that the fear of marijuana, as promoted by the 1936 film "Reefer Madness," was overblown, to say the least. Within a couple of years after its introduction, pot became an accepted alternative to drinking. Still, the overwhelming majority preferred the varieties offered by alcohol.

Because Morehouse was an extremely private place, students could pretty much do what they wanted as long as they were discreet. It was unthinkable that police would ever enter upon our campus. However, if such an event occurred, most of us decided to protect one another from any intrusions by those who were not part of our corps. Therefore, while there was no sense that anyone smoking marijuana was breaking any laws (though clearly laws were being broken), no reefer-related scandal visited upon the college during this period.

Above Our Heads

3

15 Nov 67

Dear Folks,

    This letter is to tell you how much I appreciated the gift you sent commemorating my birthday.
    I'm doing well! Am glad to hear Marvin and Billy successfully recovered from their illness. How are McKinley and Aunt Theda doing?
    When this letter reaches you Homecoming will have been underway. Anticipate it eagerly as my midterm exams will have been completed, hence, a temporary dismissal of pressure will enable me to enjoy myself.
    My grades have not been outstanding with the exception of an "A+" which I received today for my speech (final) in Public Speaking. I really am quite tired at the end of a day and I believe that my job is a major contributing factor. Yet, I am making all attempts to maintain it and the rest of my activities. You see, I am somewhat imposing upon myself pressures in a test to see what I can take. Of course I do not want to sacrifice myself in regard to academics, but it's something I want to do. I do not know my other grades otherwise I would list them.
    I do not know when I expect to leave here for Christmas, however, I anticipate paying my own fare. Thank you.

Love,
Spencer

The Making of a Morehouse Man

The cafeteria job was beginning to take its toll. It was the first job where I had an early morning obligation as well as one late in the day. It felt like I was squeezing school between my work commitments. Nevertheless, the food was good and plentiful, the surroundings attractive and I was becoming part of the kitchen staff. What we had together felt like a family. While some of us were students at Morehouse (curiously, no Spelman students worked in the kitchen, only on the serving line), the majority of employees were simply citizens of Atlanta. A couple of the guys, who were college-aged, were what Morehouse students called "Block Boys" because they were viewed as persons who "hung out on the block" or street.

Known as "townies" on other college campuses, where the college might be the major community enterprise, these were young men who could not or chose not to attend college and would make a livelihood by whatever means were available. If they chose to attend school, they would enroll at Clark or Morris Brown, perceived then to be less pretentious schools of the Atlanta University Center. They dressed in the hip street style of that day: Italian-knit shirts, sharkskin "high-water" trousers, Florsheim cap-toed shoes and stingy-brimmed straw or felt hats. The "problem" that students had with these fellows was their obvious dislike for Morehouse. They would often posture threateningly to students who would walk around town away from campus. At times there would be fights but nothing more. On rare occasions, Block Boys would come on to the campus in hot pursuit of one student or another whose looks he found objectionable.

For the most part, these guys were harmless. Because of our prejudices towards them, we simply chose to distance ourselves from them. This was where the cafeteria job was helpful. I got to know a couple of these fellows and found that they, for the most part, thought and felt about the same stuff as any man in his late teens and early 20s: women, partying, sports, movies, entertainers, money, not necessarily in that order. The resentment toward Morehouse, though, was very real.

Their understanding of us was that we thought we were better than they were. How they could come to believe this was completely understandable. We were being taught to believe that we could conquer the world. Unfortunately, this new-found sense of who we were often took a direction unintended by our mentors: setting ourselves above those who were not a part of our program. It was for this reason that a number of Morehouse students would be the object of derision that could easily lead to violence.

I also found out something else. Many of these guys who put us down wanted desperately to attend Morehouse. They knew its meaning throughout Atlanta - that Morehouse men were leaders who made things happen. Some could not gain admittance because of poor high school transcripts. Yet, the many who had no academic reasons precluding admission were reluctant to apply because they believed that they would not be "accepted" by students already in attendance. Instead, they would enter Morris Brown or Clark College and forego what they anticipated as a hassle at the 'House. Contrary to this perception, however, was the reality that those who entered Morehouse were as accepted as anyone else. The fact that you were there, with rare exceptions, sealed your relationship with the body. The distinction was further blurred between "town and gown" for another reason as well. Most Atlantans tended to commute, living at home with parents.

The Making of a Morehouse Man

This cut the annual cost of school by 50 percent. The campus population was essentially a collection of out-of-towners who were just happy to be there. Thankfully, fraternity life and athletics were two of the greatest opportunities for genuine integration. After that it was the precious spirit of Morehouse that bound "each son the other into ties more brotherly."

Above Our Heads

4

Jan. 8, 1968

Dear Folks,

So far nothing has resulted from the investigation concerning my stolen goods. It appears that they don't know what they are going to do in the event that my clothing is not recovered.

As far as that extra $50 is concerned you can forget having to pay that. It seems that they lost the card I filled out indicating the fact that at the beginning of the semester I dropped a course which would have cost $60- extra. You see, I had initially registered for twenty (20) hours. I now take seventeen (17). Any hours over the normal 17 cost $20 per hour. Hence, those three extra hours totaled $60.00. After my $10.00 fee for reservation of the room was deducted the cost was the $50 extra we saw indicated on the slip at home. Therefore, after I get another card filled out to replace the first I will not be billed. This I plan to do on Tuesday (the 9th) because I could not find the teacher whose course I dropped.

For the remainder of the semester and possibly next semester I will be living at the Newman House. It appears that the burglaries in my dormitory are increasing every day I have been back (and amounts of $50 to $100 have been taken in cash and goods each time). The Newman House is a place where college Catholics congregate for group discussions and the like. I have a room with one other fellow which includes a telephone and good heating conditions (something I didn't always get at Mays Hall. The rent is $4.00 a week payable whenever you (me) want to

The Making of a Morehouse Man

pay. I am using my fraternity brother's meal book who took my job at Spelman. He is on a scholarship which pays for room and board at Morehouse and consequently cannot get a refund on a meal book. So since I gave him my job he in turn gave me his meal book. The house has a living room, dining room and kitchen, library, office which the priest uses, chapel and two bedrooms (also two baths). Three of us live here; the other two are Catholic. I am the first Protestant to live here. I imagine I was taken on good faith. It is quite an ideal place for getting one's studying done and very private. The atmosphere is one of great concentration (this is perhaps instilled because the priest Father Graham is here quite a lot).

I mentioned that two bedrooms exist and that three of us live here. I possibly will move into the second bedroom after the fellow living there now leaves. This is expected around the end of the semester, for he will be transferring to some school in Louisiana (no, not Southern). I have proven myself a responsible individual. I will be permitted to live here next semester in the single room at the same price: $4.00 a week.

Until further notice just send the price of tuition for students living off-campus for the 2nd semester. This is in one of my catalogues or I will send it soon if you don't have it. By the way the address is Spencer Gibbs, 87 Chestnut Street, S.W., Atlanta, Georgia 30314. It is closer to campus than Bennet Hall was last semester (2nd semester Spring). This is all for now.

Love,
Spencer

P.S. Please send my desk lamp (the Tensor). It's by the safe under the bottom shelf of the bookcase in my room. Would you please send that red night shirt with U. of Oklahoma written on it. Momma does not wear it anymore and it's of no use there. Besides I need something to sleep in, I only have one pair of pajamas.

Returning to Morehouse for finals, prior to the beginning of the second semester of my junior year, was a true letdown. Upon entering my room at Mays Hall, I discovered that all of my clothing had been stolen. For the most part these were the same suits, trousers and sweaters I had brought when I first entered 2 years earlier. I felt like all people who have been burglarized: violated and angry. The school let me down in that their response was one of helplessness. At the time, the loss of three suits, four pairs of trousers and three sweaters seemed like a lot about which to be miffed. My parents were angrier than I. They engaged in a campaign of letter-writing and phone calling of school officials to no avail; their efforts simply compounded the agony, heightening everyone's frustration. Needless to say, I contacted police, filled out all kinds of claim forms and got no satisfaction. After that experience, whenever I went home for holidays, I took everything I valued with me.

The late Sixties represented transitional years for Morehouse. After 100 years of relative obscurity, it was coming into the light. The more people learned about the college and its mission, the more people were drawn to it. During this time there was an explosion of diversity. Everyone who entered did not necessarily embrace the easy-going, unhurried, trusting, community-nurturing style of life that had been Morehouse. In point of fact, some bad apples were starting to spoil the barrel. After this theft, I

The Making of a Morehouse Man

became more and more aware of the security issues that began to quickly emerge. There were enough criminal incidents occurring that I was able to convince my parents that the time had come for me to move off campus. Fantastic!

On one level, I did not want to leave the campus. It had become home and I felt as though I was being chased out of it. On the other hand, I would be moving to a location about three blocks off campus, not as far away as Bennet Hall, and in a non-institutional facility. The Newman House turned out to be a wonderful place to live. I shared a room with Malcolm Beech, a Roman Catholic from New York City, who was one of two students who also served as caretakers in exchange for a room. The Newman House, a fixture on college campuses throughout America, was a place the Roman Catholic Church provided for Catholic students to come for counseling, socializing, meditation and prayer services. Except for offering meals, it was much like the Canterbury House, with the further exception that the latter did not focus just upon Episcopalian students. Indeed, my Protestant presence at the Newman House represented a break from tradition. It was at the invitation of Malcolm that I was able to room there for the semester.

The location at the corner of Beckwith and Chestnut Streets placed it practically at the crossroads that connected the six institutions comprising the AUC. Chestnut was a lovely treelined street that I had traversed many times. Yet, now from the vantage of the Newman House porch, where we could sit for hours at a time, the street took on a special significance. Perhaps it was because I was really experiencing it, not just traversing it. It is remarkable how the memories of being on that porch could be so

Above Our Heads

precious to me now.

After a while, my presence at the Newman House began to draw other persons who had no interest whatsoever in the purposes for which it was provided. Largely, my chapter brothers would come to visit, particularly on a Friday or Saturday afternoon when classes ended for the week. There we would gather on that wonderful porch and suddenly Newman House was transformed into the Pi Chapter House. As these gatherings continued into the semester, with the weather becoming warmer and warmer, many of our female acquaintances walking by would be invited to stop and have a beer from the omnipresent keg or tub of longnecks. Soon Kappas from the other two chapters would learn of these informal times and found their way to Beckwith and Chestnut.

Before they had developed into the lively gatherings that they were to become, Roland Chevalir from Arvaudvill, Louisiana, moved out as the result of having transferred to a school in his home state. His move had absolutely nothing to do with what was developing, so, we parted friends. Malcolm's subsequent move was more difficult to accept, because he was a true "funster." We knew that he had been dating a young woman in a very serious relationship. So when he informed me that he was leaving to marry her, I felt badly that I would be losing such a good housemate. In any event, I was soon the only resident there.

Brothers would stay overnight from time to time since there was now an empty bedroom available. Living across the street from Atlanta University, I had come to know a completely new grouping of people that also included Kappas who were graduate students there. They were attracted by the obvious fun that we

The Making of a Morehouse Man

were having and began to hang out on weekends with the rest of us. Soon thereafter, parties started going into the wee hours of the morning. Because this was an older crowd, we had the opportunity to interact socially with more mature men and women whose hours away were not restricted by meddlesome dorm moms. This was the first time that some of us had ever experienced a date that included breakfast the next morning. What was most remarkable is how extraordinarily natural all of this was becoming. If my innocence had not abandoned me by now, it rushed to the exit after these experiences.

Before any of these events started happening, Father Graham had begun to be less and less of a presence on our side of town, choosing instead to carry out his work at Emory's Newman House. Because the revelry was limited to the weekends, I would be able to clean out the house after each gathering of people, not wanting to bring our festivities to the attention to the priest. If Father Graham suspected that anything was going on out of the ordinary, he never said so. The sad reality was that the Roman Catholic campus ministry was clearly going nowhere. While the House was completely available for the use of the campus ministry, any activities that occurred were generally limited to between Sunday and the following Friday. And, as time went on, even these days witnessed no activities specifically geared to the religious and spiritual needs of the Roman Catholics on campus. Parties, which could have happened at anytime throughout the week, were only allowed to occur in the first place because it was a known fact that the priest never scheduled anything during Friday afternoon through Sunday. Before the middle of the semester concluded, he eventually was not scheduling much of anything during the week.

Above Our Heads

5

Jan. 30, 1968

Dear Folks,

  The money for the second semester is due no later than Friday, Feb. 2, 1968. Total amount is $375. I did poorly for the first semester. Try not to be too upset. I intend to make up for this discrepancy in the second semester. At any rate I will not fail you. I know you don't have to send me to school. I appreciate it more than I can say. Sometimes minor problems arise which often make it difficult to progress. However, in moving to the Newman House I am really eliminating more than I can name. I am certain that everything will work out for the best.

Love,
Spencer

P.S. Send money directly to the school in form of certified check.
P.P.S. I can do without a suit. You can put the money to better use.

By my living off-campus, I saved my parents over half of what they would normally expect to pay for a room on campus. The tuition of $375 equaled the cost of housing in a residence hall. When my father realized how much was being saved, I am certain that he began to wonder why living off-campus had not been considered earlier. One reason was that fresh-

The Making of a Morehouse Man

men in 1965 had to live on campus and were subject to a curfew. By the next academic year, '66-'67, the curfew was relaxed. Yet, most students in all four classes lived on-campus. Then there simply was not the proliferation of off-campus housing options that exist today. The Newman House, a moderately-sized brick building, was among the better built houses in a neighborhood characterized by old frame housing stock. The choices available to students were often only attractive because they were off-campus, offered fewer amenities and were, therefore, usually inexpensive.

As things turned out, I did perform well in the second semester despite the new lifestyle it represented. I was now in the last semester before what I was hoping would be my last year at Morehouse. This was to be my most enjoyable semester at college. I had come to know my capabilities and was increasingly more comfortable with my development. I was also becoming more socially adept and discovering that I had a wide variety of interests. Having edited an award-winning literary magazine gave me a small bit of notoriety. I was being seen as somewhat of a bohemian type, especially by maintaining a residence off-campus. Aside from visits by fraternity brothers, I also informally hosted my friends who shared similar academic interests. Actually, these Friday afternoon gatherings were comprised of a small number of students from Spelman, Morehouse, Clark, Morris Brown and Atlanta University who were in the humanities and arts, many of whom I met by virtue of my being an English major. Through them I gained exposure to their disciplines, which broadened my own horizons. Many of these persons had experienced the Canterbury House of our freshman year and were accustomed to having free-flowing discussions on whatever topics we would

Above Our Heads

choose.

As in all areas of life, music was undergoing a major transition. Avant-garde was the term being used to identify this emerging musical style that was challenging traditions in jazz, rock and rhythm and blues. The larger cultural changes ushered in by increased drug use, flower children, and psychedelia of all types promoted new creativity while acting iconoclastically upon that which was tried, true and familiar. For example, the music of Miles Davis, whom I believed at the time to be the most accomplished jazz trumpeter of the modern era, evolved from be-bop to avant-garde. Miles led this transition among jazz musicians when his album *Bitches Brew* was released. In rock and R&B, it was Jimi Hendrix and Sly and the Family Stone. But Hendrix led the pack, influencing not just musicians of his genre, but jazz music as well. His compositions "Purple Haze," "Are You Experienced?" "Machine Gun," "The Wind Cried Mary" and others defined an era in American music that continues to exert influence to the present time.

On what was then Hunter Street, now Martin Luther King, Jr. Blvd, was located a real funky coffeehouse called "The Loving Spoonful," that played the avant-garde music of Miles and Jimi, as well as James Brown, Sly and others. The place was appropriately lit with "black lights" that made the psychedelic posters look that much more surreal than they already were. Everybody who went was hip or wanted to be hip. Of course, you could obtain marijuana as well as beer, wine and hard liquor, even though the owner had no liquor license. Atlanta was still a small town that paid little attention to the goings-on in the southwest quadrant where the Black university community existed. White Atlanta, including the police, either were in denial as to our existence or simply recognized that we were small potatoes and ignored us outright. This was fine with us. We saw their involvement in our settings as an intrusion at best and a violation of our sacred space at worst. So we could pretty much love and live as we were led.

Many was the night that my friends and I would return to the Newman House after an evening at the Loving Spoonful and carouse the rest of the night. This was the era of free love and before the advent of life-threatening sexually transmitted disease. Our biggest fear then was "getting someone pregnant." While there was a predisposition on the part of both men and women that, if the circumstances were right, sexual activity would occur, after an evening at the "Spoonful," it usually did.

ABOVE OUR HEADS

6

Mar. 11, 1968

Dear Folks,

I was looking through my drawer and came across the letter that accompanied that $25- check you sent last week. I'm writing to tell you I got the $50- and the $25-. I wasn't sure (and still I'm not) if I had written a word of thanks and recognition for the money sent at that time.
Doing okay otherwise.
Cost of transportation for trip: $80.00 round trip. Cost of room and board: $80 (approx.). I think I'll just forget it! Probably stay here or visit University of Illinois with frat brothers here if they drive up.

Love,
Spencer

Some time before the event was to occur, my fraternity brothers and I were considering attending the annual Kappa Karnival held on the campus of Southern Illinois University. This was a major social event involving Black students who were Greek as well as non-Greeks. I had not attended in the year-and-a-half that I had been a fraternity member. I was encouraged to go because at this time I was in a long-distance romance with a woman who was attending school in Chicago. She was excited, as was I, about meeting in what was for us a novel and "happen-

The Making of a Morehouse Man

ing" setting. Because of this I wanted my parents to come through with the travel money, therefore I notified them way in advance of the April 5th date on which the event was to occur. Everyone in the midwest knew about Kappa Karnival at SIU and was anticipating this one to be a better event than the one the year before. I did not want to miss it.

On the very evening that we were preparing to drive to Carbondale where SIU is situated, tragedy struck. Atlanta, as indeed the nation and world, had just begun to receive reports on the assassination of the Rev. Dr. Martin Luther King, Jr., while he was preparing to lead a garbage workers' strike in Memphis. I fear that many of us, at first hearing this news, did not understand the enormous gravity of the moment. Some of us, myself included, thought that we could still make the Carbondale trip. But it became evident that King's death was not something to be regarded as momentary.

It is important to understand the context of April 4, 1968. While King was an important civil rights figure, he was not the enormous historical figure then that he was to become. Before his death, King was viewed by many as one among a host of civil rights figures, all of whom enjoyed a great measure of prominence. For this was a time when one could pick and choose from a smorgasbord of persons leading the quest for civil rights. There was Malcolm X, Stokely Carmichael, Fannie Lou Hamer, Ralph Abernathy, James Bevel, Shirley Chisholm, Bayard Rustin, and so many others. Therefore, while Martin's loss was a dramatic blow to the Movement, it was not believed then that his death would slow its momentum to a virtual standstill.

A mood of devastation and loss that emerged from the Black

community that night in Atlanta was preceded by rage. The streets slowly, and then ever more quickly, began to fill with students and other citizens, shouting protests and beginning a campaign to desecrate all things owned or associated with white persons, as is the case with all urban-based uprisings against the unjust social order that has continued to victimize Black people. Yet Atlanta's reaction did not result in the pervasive acts of violence to property within the Black community itself, which was the response to his death in other cities. Instead, the mood gradually turned from rage to thoughtful concern. The colleges, particularly Morehouse, led the community in assembling students in prayer vigils that night. Astute faculty members seeing the need to control emotions and the opportunity to invite purposeful introspection, helped to create a climate of relative calm.

After attending one of these prayer meetings, I returned home that evening in a very meditative mood. I had long since abandoned the notion of going to SIU for the weekend and instead entered the living room, started a fire in the fireplace and settled back on to my sofa to think. I was hoping that full-scale insurrection was not going to occur throughout Atlanta. The noises outside my door along Chestnut Street seemed to be escalating. I thought about how, in a cruel way, the debate raging over who made the most sense out of the freedom struggle - Martin or Malcolm - was now over. I did not realize how powerful a statement Martin King's death, more so perhaps even than his life, would make in the days and years to come. Suddenly, I was lurched from my thoughts by a knock on the door.

A good friend that I had not seen for some time was standing on my porch. With him were two women who were crying. My

The Making of a Morehouse Man

buddy, Malcolm Beech, sheepishly uttered something about how crazy the world was and asked if they were interrupting me from something, coming unannounced? I quickly ushered them in and, upon seeing my fire going, they began to feel better. Malcolm had brought his fiancé and her friend to dinner at Paschal's and while there heard the news about King and saw Hunter Street begin to react. My place was only a short distance so they came by, more for a friendly safe place to wait it out rather than an intended visit.

It had started to rain and the nighttime with the fire going made my living room all the more pleasant.

"Why did this have to happen?" Maude, Malcolm's wife wondered aloud, speaking to no one in particular.

"Because he was getting too close," Malcolm quickly replied.

"Too close to what?" Dolores, Maude's friend, inquired.

"He was coming to understand the interrelationship of the two major events taking place in the world right now, Vietnam and the American civil rights movement." Indeed, Martin had uttered pronouncements against the War in Vietnam exactly one year ago from the day of his assassination and people began to wonder by what authority had he done so. After all, Vietnam was the issue of white peaceniks, flower children and hippies, not of a Black civil rights leader. Similarly, Malcolm X began to discover that followers of Islam came in all colors and he had begun to tone down his characteristically vitriolic tirades against white people. To be sure, both leaders believed that the unjust conditions suffered by Black people were the direct result of white racism. Yet, by now they were evolving in their understanding of the human condition to see that there could exist a complexity of fac-

Above Our Heads

tors causing the violence, in all of its forms, daily visited upon people of color. If Black people were colored in the eyes of Martin, then, so too were the Vietnamese. All of us were victims of a global system of institutionalized racism that only sought to keep Europe and her worldwide descendants in power. And if there could be white people who loved Allah, as Malcolm had come to learn, then individual white people had to be judged on their merits rather than on the basis of skin color alone.

"And because he got too close to the truth, they took him out," Malcolm concluded rather resoundingly. This was followed by a long pregnant pause until, fighting against my own impending sense of depression, I stood and blurted out, "What are we going to do? We're here together, we have one another, let's enjoy the moment." With that, Malcolm reached into his book bag, pulled out a bottle of rum and asked, "Got any butter, Spencer?"

I went into the kitchen, bringing glasses, cinnamon, nutmeg and a stick of butter. What better way to warm us from a wet and cool night than with hot buttered rums, a drink that had become popularized from an Isaac Hayes recording named after the drink. We continued to talk and consider the future, not knowing what lay ahead in the days to come. As long as I made grades, at least I would not have to worry about being drafted, at least not until after graduation a year from then. So, we enjoyed the night, the fire and the rum and I made new friends.

7

April 29, 1968

Dear Folks,

  I am doing well. Received last allowance. Has income tax return arrived yet? Impatiently await! Still want to go to California but intend to come home first. Perhaps be home on or before May 30th. Patty Powell called the Director of Housing, Mr. West, in an attempt to reach me. But my roommate had his phone taken out when he moved. I have another roommate, however. At any rate please send information leading to the whereabouts of said named individual - Patty Powell.
  My roommate Malcolm got married last week. He's a junior still at Morehouse. My new roommate Theodric Harrel, is a frat brother of mine and from Chicago. He'll remain here this summer (in Atlanta at the Newman House).
  Are you enjoying the organ? I hope someone can play it when I come home. All for now.

Love,
Spencer

The campus was the site of the funeral held for Dr. Martin Luther King, Jr. The contrast between the day on which it was held and the night of his death was vivid. The chaotic and frightening night that was April 4, 1968, was now replaced by a solemnity and calm that was amazing in light of the huge numbers of persons who had gathered. Of course, celebri-

Above Our Heads

ties from all over the world who had personally known Martin gathered at Morehouse to pay their final respects to a man who was becoming a giant with every passing moment. Most prominent among those present that day were Sammy Davis, Jr., Diana Ross, Mahalia Jackson, Hubert H. Humphrey, Harry Belafonte, Richard M. Nixon, Stokely Carmichael and the surviving Kennedy brothers, Bobby and Edward. Many of King's colleagues and co-workers who would gain national recognition in later years were also present to witness what the 1968 Torch described as "The King Comes Home." Among these persons, all of whom had a special and unique relationship to King, included James Bevel, Andrew Young and Ralph Abernathy.

Every member of the student body was invited to be a part of the funeral procession, which began at Ebenezer Baptist Church on Auburn Avenue in downtown Atlanta and wound through those narrow streets to Morehouse. We marched together, arm-in-arm, with fellow students, friends, and unknown others who had converged on the church and whom we met along the way following a mule-driven, simple farming wagon carrying King's rough-hewn wooden casket. This was clearly the largest gathering Atlanta had ever witnessed, notwithstanding the popularity of its sports stadiums, with estimates of more than 200,000 persons filling the streets and grounds that comprised Morehouse.

At the invitation of Benjamin E. Mays, then the immediate past president of Morehouse, the funeral service was held in the quadrangle of the college because Ebenezer, one of King's former pulpits, could not accommodate the large crowd that was anticipated. The "front" of the assembly was the steps leading up to Harkness Hall, the Atlanta University-owned building that also contained the Morehouse administrative offices, over which was built a huge speaker's platform. Even though with speaker after speaker the service was lengthy, we students were energetically riveted to all that we heard and saw. We wrestled with competing emotions of pain and pride, honor and horror, to be a part of this enormous gathering commemorating the life of one who was viewed by "outsiders" as a national leader but one whom we, Morehouse Men, regarded as our fallen brother.

Early on in that day some students had decided not to march or participate in any way with the King funeral. Among those who took this position were those who did not respect King's nonviolent methodology of protest, favoring instead the "by any means necessary" philosophy of Malcolm X. Yet, when the funeral processional arrived on campus, one could see students who were dressed in casual clothes rushing to their dorm rooms, to re-emerge in a matter of minutes in an appropriate dark suit, now only too willing to join the rest of us as we lined the quadrangle, defined by Harkness Hall to the east, the towering roofline of Graves Hall to the west, Benjamin Mays' stately president's home to the north and the row of science buildings and Sale and Robert Hall to the south.

From all of these events we finally began to understand the gravity of this man's influence upon the world. His assassination was as important, if not more important, than the John F. Kennedy murder of less than five years earlier. Rev. Ralph Abernathy, who was one of many delivering eulogies that day, said it best. Basing his remarks on the Joseph story in Genesis, he concluded that while you can kill the dreamer, you can't kill the dream. In a curious way, King's life and work were eclipsed by his death. For he will ever stand as a symbol of the fight to end human oppression, not just as it impacts upon Black America, but upon the human family.

After the dust began to settle and life returned to its normal rhythm, the school resumed, fully recharged, with its mission of training men. Around the middle of the semester, my fraternity brother Theodric Harrel, also from Chicago, asked if he could move in to the Newman House and live there for the remainder of the semester. Once this occurred, our brothers really did begin to believe that the place had become a Kappa House and began to wonder why a plaque showing our Greek letters was not affixed to the building. When Theodric or "The" (rhymes with see) arrived, even some of his buddies from his class who were not in the fraternity would visit. Upon visiting us, these non-fraternity men began to believe that Kappa was somehow more fun than the other fraternities. The house unintentionally became one of the greatest recruiting tools the chapter had ever had. When I pledged, there were twelve brothers in Pi. This number increased to around sixty on the eve of my graduation. At that time there were two pledge classes per year. That spring, the line was about 15 strong, a respectable demonstration of interest.

With the departure of Roland and Malcolm, the last Roman Catholic students to reside in the Newman House, and the priest shifting the emphasis away from southwest Atlanta, support for the house's continuing presence by the Roman Catholic Church was dwindling quickly. I had no way of knowing at that time that the Newman House would be sold to Morehouse and become the headquarters for the Institute of the Black World the following year. However, when I no longer began seeing Father Graham in

The Making of a Morehouse Man

the last month or so of the semester and neither The or myself paid any more rent, I sensed that something was afoot. Still, we were allowed to live there without worry that the lights, water or gas would be shut off, since we were protecting the church's property interest. With this turn of events, needless to say, my last month or so of my junior year was a blast.

Around this time I met Micky Henderson, a Morehouse graduate and frat brother who had become a naval officer. While in college, he was a member of the swim team and could swim like a fish. At this time he had been assigned to duty in Atlanta as a Navy recruitment officer. Micky had grown up in Atlanta and was living in his mother's home or she was living with him, I was never certain of the arrangement. Yet, from all appearances he seemed to be in charge because he was always having festive gatherings of Morehouse and Spelman students in his home anytime that he wanted. We hit it off instantly. He was like a breath of fresh air. Micky was a truly giving brother who let me borrow his car whenever he was not using it. He owned a fire engine red 1966 Volkswagen Beetle, identical to one my father had purchased. This, naturally, reminded me of home. Since I was becoming familiar to his family, they became like a second family, and he, like the big brother I never had.

As the time for college graduation neared in schools all over America, I was asked to deliver a gift of an automobile to Dr. J.B. Harris' daughter, Sylvia Ann. Actually, Victor Wright, whose family was intimately connected to the Harrises, was asked by Dr. Harris to find a responsible Morehouse man to help Vic deliver the car to his daughter. J.B., a physician, was a Morehouse grad, class of 1925, and married to one of the few women who received

ABOVE OUR HEADS

a Morehouse degree. Dottie, who graduated in 1936, was one of only 26 women able to attend Morehouse because of a rare historical event. Until this time, Atlanta University maintained both an undergraduate and graduate program. However, the administration, upon deciding to phase out the undergraduate degree program, entered into an agreement with Morehouse and Spelman to allow the A.U. undergraduate men to complete their bachelor's degrees by matriculating at the men's school and the women to complete their work at the women's. Because Dottie had taken a number of courses at Morehouse while a student at A.U., she was allowed to finish her studies at Morehouse, and thus was one of a handful of females to graduate from the college in the '30s because of this temporary policy.

So, at the end of the school year I found myself behind the wheel of a brand new 1968 Ford Galaxy, following behind Victor in his MGB on the road to Fisk University in Nashville, where Sylvia Ann was graduating. I found it somewhat remarkable that this doctor with whom I had had only the most brief encounter, would trust me to deliver this expensive graduation gift to his daughter. Vic and I talked about it: I reasoned that it was solely because of Victor's relationship to the family. Vic insisted that it was because I was a Morehouse man. This is when he told me that J.B. insisted that Vic's choice be a Morehouse student and not one of the many others of his friends' sons then living in Atlanta. By now it was becoming wholly evident that the Morehouse emblem, once stamped upon you, made you "good to go" unless your own actions proved otherwise.

The Making of a Morehouse Man

YEAR FOUR

"There is an air of Expectancy at Morehouse College. It is expected that the student who enters here will do well. It is also expected that once a man bears the insignia of a Morehouse Graduate, he will do exceptionally well. We expect nothing less...
May you perform so well that when a man is needed for an important job in your field, your work will be so impressive that the committee of selection will be compelled to examine your credentials. May you forever stand for something noble and high. Let no man dismiss you with a wave of the hand or a shrug of the shoulder..."

The Charge to the Graduating
Class of 1961
Benjamin Elijah Mays
President, Morehouse College

Above Our Heads

The Making of a Morehouse Man

1

19 Nov. 68

Dear Folks,

I am doing well but could be a lot better. Thank you very much for remembering me at the time of my birthday. The gift I received was the most practical one I got (which by the way, was the only one!!). I received the box and was thankful for that also as it saved me from starvation many a night. Yesterday I finished my mid-semester examinations. I believe I did fairly well but retain enough doubt as I cannot really predict any grades. As soon as I receive them I will inform you.

Upon receiving your last letter I must say I was somewhat amused. Even though Marvin's actions were somehow not in keeping with what is expected of all of us it did happen; this goes to show that the best of moral teachings and/or disciplinarian attitudes do not always insure the best in youth. There is a definite need for compassion and humanity and understanding when attempting to make someone what you would want to be proud of.

I have a telephone now. The number is 523-5259. The area code is 404.

I have been considering moving again. The philosophy of the fraternity house has not been realized. Here I am 21 years old and I am still being treated just as the seventeen year old freshman student. Here I have been for the last three and one-half years and it seems as though this has had no effect on those people in administrative positions. Here I am making satisfactory progress toward a degree and I'm given the same treatment as one who is on probation. Here I am a fraternity man (and this is supposed to be an honorable position since one has to have a certain average to become a part of one) and I'm given the same benefits as the man who has not even been given time to amass an average! And if a man happens to be a relative of, or good friend, or even a frat brother to one of the administrators of Morehouse College he can be obtaining an average of 1.0 consecutively for every semester here at Morehouse and still graduate with his class. I, personally, know of several cases like this (one being from Chicago whose godfather is Mr. J. A. Lockett). For these reasons I feel that the policies of this school concerning the sociological atmosphere it possesses is wholly unfair and for the most part totally undemocratic. Regardless, however, whether I move off campus or not I am in the process of writing a manuscript of some length, expressing my views, in connection with another person who possesses similar beliefs.

    What is Dee's address in Baltimore? I plan to go there for Christmas as the fraternity will have its National (or Grand) Chapter meeting in that city. If I went I would like to stay at Dee's since she did invite me once before. The fraternity meeting will begin on the 26th of December and last until the 28th. So it is possible for me to come home first, if you like, which would be about the 20th or 21st and then leave there on the morning of the 26th and go to Baltimore. After the conclave I could return or either visit Loleta or tour the East Coast as many of my brothers here desire to do.

    I have applied to Boston University School of Law

The Making of a Morehouse Man

and University of Iowa College of Law. I will still make application to Columbia University and George Washington. I have enclosed a scholarship form which I want you to fill out and return to me or mail to this address:

    Director of Admissions
    University Hall
    The University of Iowa
    Iowa City, Iowa 52240

Make corrections on the application as you see fit.

I did receive check for tuition (receipt is enclosed). I have been thinking seriously of going to the Peace Corps. I cannot see myself getting accepted to law school and then after two months being drafted, after paying all that money and wasting time. Then too, the Peace Corps has many benefits:

1) People coming out of the Peace Corps usually are granted fellowships if they plan to do graduate work as these people have a great deal to contribute to the academic world.

2) The experience gained as well as the knowledge and travel that is to be derived is received at no cost to you or myself.

3) I feel that I would rather do something worthwhile and humane than to support something which is senseless as well as destructive with no logical end in sight (Vietnam and the entire U.S.A. position on poverty, people and peace).

4) There are perhaps many others; I consider these to be the foremost.

Sorry for the delay in writing but I don't like to write anyone if I don't have something worthwhile to relay.

                                      Spencer

Above Our Heads

Since the fraternities had grown in size considerably in the last few years, even witnessing the founding of a fifth independent fraternal organization, Phi Lambda, within that time period, the college acceded to the wishes of the Pan Hellenic Council by granting its request to convert the buildings of Quarles Court into fraternity houses. With the exception, for unknown reasons, of Phi Lambda, the national fraternities of Alpha Phi Alpha, Kappa Alpha Psi, Phi Beta Sigma and Omega Psi Phi were each given the use of buildings for their chapter houses. Even though the school retained ownership and our room payment arrangement went unchanged, this signaled that for the first time in the school's history Greek life was finally being openly embraced by the school's administration in allowing this highly visible presence on campus. The school's former president, Benjamin Mays, who had retired after the academic year 1966-67, did not believe that fraternities at Morehouse were helpful to the educational process. Many of the faculty also shared this view. Therefore, Greeks for all these years had been simply tolerated as necessary evils. Ironically, this position was held even though Mays had earlier been initiated into the membership of Omega Psi Phi. Yet, like so many who had gone through the grinder of pledging, the fraternity lost its luster for many who would later sever themselves from their fraternal bonds.

When I returned to Morehouse for my fourth and what I hoped would be my final year, I moved into the Kappa House. As coincidence would have it, the room to which I was assigned was the very room in which I began my college career: Room 208, Building or Unit Five of Quarles Court. The former Units, now fraternity chapter houses, were situated behind Graves Hall,

The Making of a Morehouse Man

slightly to the south of it and immediately adjacent to what was then the college infirmary. A walkway, leading to the rear of Samuel H. Archer Hall, our physical education building, separated the infirmary from the court. The school permitted each chapter to decorate, at its own expense, its house as it saw fit. No one flew to this task more quickly than Donald Hense, my line brother from the Fall of 1966. He took complete control of the redecoration project. By all accounts he did a good job, as soon a plush crimson carpet covered the floor of the small common room that we designated our "den." Hense engaged a carpenter to create a wooden radiator cover that turned our heating unit into what looked like an attractive piece of furniture. The walls were painted cream which, together with the carpet, comprised the fraternity's colors. He then went on to purchase some decent furniture, which when installed, made our house the talk of the campus. Once installed, he became like a mother hen in relation to that room, so protective was he of his accomplishment. Soon after the area was completed and for a long time thereafter, upon entering it, I was led to feel as if I was in the more formal living room of my parents' home. He enforced his own code of what type of behavior was appropriate for the den and would attempt to monitor activities which might result in damage.

Hense was a student of older years and could be quite impatient with the conduct of his younger brothers (which were all of us), unless we marched locked-step to his directives. His impatience found its zenith in me. As we were both seniors, we were naturally viewed as leaders by our chapter brothers. Yet, he was far more determined to lead because he was by this time a very astute political animal. He possessed a *savoir-faire* that only comes with age. He knew how to get what he wanted and he stopped at nothing until he prevailed. This, I was to learn later, was a necessary trait to have in the business world, but of questionable merit in the close-knit life of a fraternity chapter house.

In my case, he demonstrated his influence upon the college housing office, who directed room assignments even in the houses, by having me removed from Room 208 and placed in a smaller room so that he and his favorite brother could room together. I was angry as hell for the longest time but learned that there was little I could do about it. I discovered that Hense had reserved the room a year before, or so he said, and that Hawes, who I thought had done the same thing on our behalf, believed that I had. It turned out that the room that I was moved to, while somewhat smaller, was on a corner and possessed a better view. It was there that I got to know my brother, James Somerville, and thus began to forge a strong fraternal bond with him that might not otherwise have happened. Yet, it was Joseph Somerville, James' older brother, who led me to take an interest in befriending him.

Joseph Somerville, while being a genuine "character," was a true campus leader. Joseph, an early admissions student, was a 1966 graduate of the college, a Kappa and president of the Student Government Association during his senior year. I got to know him when I pledged in my freshman year during his last semester. He was among the most decent, fun-loving, brightest men I had come to know. Joe Somerville drank nothing but Bacardi Rum and had a genuine love of cigars, both of which he'd indulge whenever opportunity presented itself. He was truly a man among men; no one disliked him and he was respected by students, staff and faculty alike. It was during that Spring'66

The Making of a Morehouse Man

pledge period that Joseph befriended me, taking me under his wing, helping to make pledging bearable. Instead of engaging in physical hazing upon us, as my other big brothers were prone to do, Joe compelled us to do creative projects, even though they may have been considered of little consequence in the long run. For instance, one day he asked me to draw an exact likeness of the Bacardi rum bottle label...six feet by four feet employing the same colors seen on the original. The project took a week and upon completion he proudly hung the poster-like drawing on his dorm room wall, bragging that his "pledge" created it for him. Compared to a memory of beatings, I'll hold to this one any day. It was because of these kinds of experiences with Joe that I welcomed the friendship of James.

Both James and Joseph hailed from Virginia Beach, Virginia. James pledged Kappa in the spring semester of 1967-68, while a sophomore, so though I had known him for about a year, we had not grown close. When we began rooming together, this slowly began to change. We did not take to each other instantly. Somerville was an iconoclast; he was not easily impressed with either people or institutions simply because they were regarded highly by others. Indeed, he would hold up to ridicule that which may have been tried and true just because he could. He would, from time to time, be unreasonable and intolerant of views held in opposition to his own. Yet, for whatever reasons, he came to respect me and regarded me as his brother. We began to get along very well, though we existed in marked contrast to one another. He was a southern "country boy" and proud of it (though Virginia Beach was hardly a rural town even in the '60s). Every now and then, he would lapse into an even more informal style of

Above Our Heads

behavior than was actually his manner. On the other hand, I was a northern urbanite who enjoyed a more cultivated spin on life. Yet, the old axiom was true then as it is now: opposites attract.

We introduced our friends to each other. He got to know seniors and I became acquainted with juniors and sophomores, whose paths I may never have crossed. Neither one of us knew any freshmen, it being so early in the year, nor would we be likely to, so insulated from them as we were in coursework and social life. If a man was not a member of the fraternity or on an athletic team, then seniors would not have occasion to know sophomores and freshmen. Therefore, these organizations within the college were a good device for breaking through the class barriers that were the natural circumstance of college.

The Kappa House housed 24 students. Though there were many more brothers than this in the chapter, many chose to live off campus, in other campus residences or had become married in their senior year. In any event, there were one or two spaces for non-fraternity guys to live. Early in that first semester I got to know two of these men through Somerville as they had been friends since they first entered the college as freshmen two years earlier. Neal Robinson or "Bama," as he was nicknamed, came from Montgomery Alabama, and roomed with Ron DeVerges, a Kappa from Los Angeles. Their friend, a sophomore from Gary, West Virginia, named Ed Stewart, hung out in their room so much that he may as well have lived there.

One night, Somerville and I decided to throw a party in our room. Unfortunately, we chose to use our room to hold the party. Besides the den on the first floor, which could accommodate a larger number than our room, there was the basement that we had

The Making of a Morehouse Man

converted into a party room. Nevertheless, due in large part to the spontaneity of the moment, DeVerges, Stew, Bama, Somerville, myself and an equal number of women piled into our corner room. We were playing the music of Iron Butterfly, Sly and the Family Stone, James Brown, the Beatles, Sam and Dave and others LOUDLY. Beginning around 10 p.m., after Trevor Arnett closed, we partied hearty for all of an hour, when there was an equally loud, intrusive knocking on our door. Turning the music down, an act much like closing the barn door after the horse has run out, we answered the knock. To our horror, standing in the doorway was none other than Mr. Robert West, director of housing. I'll never forget the electricity that ran through my body when he pointed a finger at me, as if stabbing the air, saying simply, "Nine o'clock! Tomorrow! My office!" He repeated this simple direction to each man in the room and then dismissed the women.

Before Mr. West had knocked on our door, Bama had left the room to retrieve something from his own and Deverges had crouched behind the opened door, shielded from West's view by it. They managed to escape West's invitation. Stew, myself and Somerville were smarting from the experience. Then, almost immediately thereafter, some brothers who knew about our party and were heading for it, stopped the women who were leaving the house to ask what was happening. They explained the events as they had happened moments before and were asked to wait outside while they came inside. John Horton Smith, or "Cochise" as he was known, who had pledged with Somerville, entered the room and explained that they had interested some people in coming to the party and that they and the women who had just left

Above Our Heads

were all downstairs waiting for the next step. We said it was too late - that West had busted us and the party was over. At that moment The, my fraternity brother who had lived with me at the Newman House, volunteered his apartment to continue the party. Somerville and I looked at each other and shrugged our shoulders as if to say "What the heck!" Since it was a five minute walk to The's house on Joyce Street and feeling we had nothing more to lose and an overwhelming need to salvage the night, we jumped at the opportunity. Of course, DeVerges felt great since he did not get caught and volunteered to buy a bottle for the "new" party. Bama, who was "innocent," was happy to come, feeling sorry for those of us caught by West, yet offering to do nothing. By the time we left to go to The's place, there were a number of people gathered. We must have looked like a midnight parade leaving campus that night.

Cochise, from Tulsa, Oklahoma, looked like a Native American, hence his nickname. His father was a well-respected educator in his hometown and a fraternity brother. Cochise, during these days, seemed to want to place distance between the strait-laced ways of his father and himself. Said another way, the younger Smith was wild. Actually, he was simply the most fun-loving guy I had ever met and was immensely popular with men and women. He was the life of every party and was earnest in his efforts at making certain that this opportunity for fun would not be lost. Thanks to him, in large part, we had an exceptionally fine time and our reputations as social animals remained intact.

This semester also represented a serious time in our lives as seniors. If we were going to get into graduate school, this was the time to apply. Despite all of the fun I was having, from the time

The Making of a Morehouse Man

of Newman House days until the present moment, my grades were not so bad as to prevent me from believing that I would not be continuing on to professional school. But I was also considering other options. One of those was the Peace Corps. I remembered a conversation I had with Herbert Holmes, a senior during my freshman year who had returned for Homecoming while I was a junior. He spoke of his time spent in the Peace Corps following graduation. Making it seem glamorous, he had been assigned to work in Mogadishu, Somalia. Holmes, who was a genius, was asked to go for a time to Accra, Ghana to teach mathematics and physics in a local high school. While there, he lived in a high-rise apartment overlooking the city and somehow was able to secure a maid and a cook, which impressed me. Being from Chicago, living in a large city in Africa, while attractive, seemed too amazingly impossible to be true. Nevertheless, no matter how appealing this seemed and even though I made application, I did not seriously pursue a possible assignment in the Peace Corps because I thought that if I was accepted it would forestall what I really wanted to do, which was to go to law school.

I talked with Nelson Taylor during this time about career choices and he too was ambivalent as to which direction he wanted to go. Nelson, my fraternity brother, was president of the Student Government Association and brilliant. For him the choices were either law school or the seminary or both. It was during this time that men at Morehouse discussed their destiny in a manner that was completely mind-boggling. For most of us, wherever you resided on the globe, we were taught to believe that a man or woman only prepared him or herself for one career in life. If you were a biology major, then of course you were either

Above Our Heads

going to become a research scientist or a medical practitioner, but certainly not both. So, Nelson's sense of the future order of a person's life was that it should not be limited to the expected. It was this single lesson that was to be the defining moment for me as to what this college was really all about. Before the expression "living outside of the box" was coined, Morehouse had created a context for its men to think about the totality of possibilities that existed for them. Soon after my exchange with Nelson, I began to have a number of conversations with others in my class who were beginning to express similar views and I recognized that it was to my advantage to acquiesce and follow them onto the path of expanded thinking.

At Morehouse, the Christmas holiday did not signal the break between semesters. Instead, the semester ended after our return from the holidays and final examinations. So there was always a tension mingled with joy during this season. While you could have fun at this time of year, there was always the nagging reality of facing exams upon your return to school. This fact made it particularly hard to consider attending the Kappa Conclave, the national meeting of the fraternity held every 18 months, either in August or December. Since this was my last year of college and I had never attended such an event, I threw caution to the wind and along with several of my chapter brothers decided to attend.

This was to be my first time in Baltimore, the site of the meeting. When we got there early in the morning of the first day, there was considerable confusion over lodging and hooking up with my brothers from Morehouse. We had all arrived by different means, some coming by bus, train or automobile. Because I had gone to Chicago for Christmas, I arrived by plane on the

The Making of a Morehouse Man

26th. For whatever reason, we felt that we all had to arrive at the Lord Baltimore Hotel, the convention site, as a unit. After missed attempts at meeting people at bus stations and train depots, we got to the hotel only to discover rooms not properly assigned. My backup plan was to stay with a family friend who I had always known as Aunt Dee, my mother's oldest friend. As it turned out, those who got rooms invited others who didn't to sleep on the floors in theirs. It was among the best times we had ever had.

The Conclave seemed to be designed for young, college-aged men and women looking to have fun. Even though Kappa is intergenerational with the majority of members being college alumni, the occasion had many events catering to us. It was reminiscent of that first province meeting in Columbus, except a thousand times bigger. I met guys from all over the country who would become good friends. Each day and evening there were socials, dances and the occasional business meeting. Food and drink were in constant abundance as were the coeds from neighboring colleges. It seemed that my whole world was coming together in this place.

Above Our Heads

2

14 Jan. 69

Dear Folks,

I am now in the midst of studying for finals. My last day of classes was today.

My telephone will probably remain disconnected for the duration of the semester as I do not have funds to reconnect it. When I had my roommate to have the phone disconnected for the holidays he told them just disconnect it. This left them with the impression that we no longer desired phone service. They in turn took the money for the last bill out of my $30.00 deposit and are sending me the remainder in the mail. I will now have to pay $30. again if I desire phone service.

My income tax return form is around the house somewhere. Please send it so that I may sign it. I had intended to take care of it but forgot.

I am scheduled to take the LSAT (Law School Admission Test) on Feb. 8. At that time I will know about my acceptance at either Iowa or Boston U. I have an application to a school in Washington, D. C., Trinity College which offers a two-year fellowship for an MAT. It pays all expenses and the participant is granted a two-year deferment. I may as well send that in also. I am waiting to hear from the Peace Corps.

I am intent on moving at the end of this semester. My self and three other students are contemplating renting in a house across the street from school. The house has seven rooms. The rent is $175- per month, or $43.75 per person. A meal book is about $30.00 per month. No more money would be spent than normally. Beginning the second semester I plan to work on Saturdays and Sundays for the Internal Revenue Service as an income tax recorder (or something similar) $1.85/hr.

Tomorrow (Jan. 15) is Martin Luther King, Jr. Day. No classes. All day memorial services at Westgate Cemetary and Ebeneezer Baptist Church. By the time you receive this you may have already watched this on T.V. (I'm not sure if this will be televised).

That's all for now.

Love,
Spencer

The day after the party, we who were requested to appear before Mr. West did so promptly at 9 a.m. I was scared to death. It was my sense that since we had broken the rule against permitting women into bedrooms, we were going to be expelled from school. I slowly resigned myself to the fact that if that occurred, I would never be able to face my parents. All of their faith in me would have been unjustified not to mention the financial expense they had undertaken to send me to school in the first place. Then, of course, there was the little matter of being killed by them if I so much as appeared within striking distance. In a way, building the worst case scenario prepared me mentally for whatever the outcome might be.

Surprisingly, Mr. West announced that he would let the Pan-Hellenic Council decide our fate. Simultaneously, I was relieved and depressed. I thought that surely my peers would understand that a guy's just got to have a little fun from time to time. It was not as though we had committed an alarming, heinous deed. It was not as though we were caught naked in compromising positions with consenting minors. Yet, their authority provided them with a variety of possible options that they could choose to exercise: they could choose to do nothing, or to recommend expulsion or choose any form of punishment lying between those two extremes.

To this day, I believe the Pan-Hell would have let us off but for one tiny element: Hense. He had gotten himself elected as our representative to the Council and when that finally came home, I had already begun to look for an off-campus location. Having me out of the house would secure his position as the resident senior brother. Apparently, the members of the Council agreed to recommend that we remain in school but that we be reassigned to other campus locations. At least the Council did not expel us from school altogether. Because Stew was not a resident of the house, he was directed to live off-campus. Somerville was removed to Robert Hall. And I was allowed to live in Mays Hall. As the incident leading to these actions occurred before the end of the semester, we were not to be relocated until the beginning of the next semester.

While I suggested to my parents in a letter I had written them that I was moving voluntarily, they were never to learn from the school that this was not the case. My parents never knew about the party and my resulting punishment. As long as I was not being expelled and the outcome did not require an outlay of additional money on their part, I reasoned that they did not need to know. It would only have needlessly upset them. Therefore, I took the whole business of it in stride. After all, I had moved to a different residence every semester that I was in college. Who knows, I reasoned, maybe all those prior moves were to prepare

The Making of a Morehouse Man

me for this one. I think that because I was considered the ringleader, I could have suffered a much worse fate. Yet, by this time I had been promoted to chief justice of the Student Court and had edited an award-winning literary magazine. My hope was that I was seen as a valuable asset to the student body and that my violation really did not warrant dismissal. I will never know, however, what reasoning was used to determine the decisions that were made. We were not allowed to argue our cases, therefore, it was West's report that was the only evidence the Council had to consider.

The chapter house was a great place to live and it absolutely lived up to my expectations for life in it. Yet, needless to say, the relationship I had with Hense deteriorated completely after this. I was so angry for so long that I wrote a poem about him in *The New Catalyst*. Everyone who read it immediately understood and empathized with my position. I have reproduced it here:

A SATIRE ON A VERY GRAND OLD MAN

> Woe be unto men who are without the
>   Common sense,
> To make amends before they get in dutch
>   With the honorable Mr. H——.
> For men and minds have long been
>   Placed in opposition,
> With a bit of manipulation and
>   Juxtaposition,
> From a grand old man who
>   Maintained position
> From a higher place than either
>   You or I.

Above Our Heads

But let us not tarry and be on
    With the tale
About how D. H. created on earth for
    Men a living Hell.
And how he was
    Through blind conceit
Able to elevate himself from among the masses,
    Standing high upon his feet.

He came here when he was
    Nigh score and four
A grand old gent who wasn't satisfied
    With having more.
But wanted all because, of course,
    It was rightfully his, a blessing from the gods,
And tried to take it with no remorse.

A way had he of making people
    Feel
That he was doing everything to
    Satisfy their will.
But actually he was fulfilling
    His own greedy wants
Ne'er shrinking away from this
    By a few's jeer and taunts
Who could see through the guise,
    Those ignobled fools.

'Twas a cold day in November
    When this man H——
Let his wrath fall like timber,
Exile did he four fellows fooled
    From the confines of his Kastle
Who were then left alone
    With a problem to wrestle

The Making of a Morehouse Man

>Of where they would go and
>   How they would carry on
>Without this heartless foe.
>
>Yet unbeknownst to them
>This too had been decided by
>   Him.
>For they could live most anywhere
>As long as it did not interrupt the lair
>Of the one so mighty as the grand
>   Mr. H——.
>
>I feel my friends that my tale
>   should perhaps end.
>It could go on and on and
>   Continue to offend
>But what is the good
>   If the present subtle meaning
>Is hardly understood.
>
>Yet the laurels of old grand D
>Shall always be remembered though
>   Perhaps will always lead
>To the evil acts he committed
>   And did breed
>The noble nature which was
>   Rightfully his.

I signed it Anonymous though everyone knew the author and who H——- was. After it was published, my anger towards Hense ceased along with the relationship. I regretted the fact that our egos clashed in such a way that there was no apparent possibility for reconciliation. It did not look good for the whole "unity thing" espoused by fraternities at that time. Yet, another lesson we were to learn is that, just as in any family, even the closest units of people will clash and create long-lived animosity.

 Living in Mays Hall in my final semester at Morehouse proved to be enjoyable. I had lived here once before as a first semester junior, but this time seemed very different. My roommate, Edward Long, had an extraordinarily biting sense of humor. We got along perfectly. Soon after we settled in, Ed, a junior from Thomson, Georgia, gave me no end of grief about being kicked out of the fraternity house. He had known about my rivalry with Hense, which was made abundantly clear after the poem appeared in *The New Catalyst*. He thought I was better off not living there. His position was that all those fraternity guys were snobs and the fact that they lived together in a dwelling separate from the other students proved it. He had never pledged a fraternity and with two years to go until graduation, saw no need to do so. When he said this, I simply chalked it up to "sour grapes." While there was a discernible tone of envy in his voice, he never mentioned it again, realizing perhaps that I cared less about his opinion about this part of college life in which I had found value.

 Ed was always good for diversion from the stress of the day, especially during this particularly trying time when a senior only had a few months in which to decide his future. When I would return to the room, often late at night, Ed invariably had a room full of his friends smoking cigarettes, drinking wine and telling lies and jokes for hours. While I knew his friends, as we were all in school together, they were his friends. So, once again, I was making "new" acquaintances because of another change in location and roommates.

 It turned out that many of Ed's buddies had held some erro-

The Making of a Morehouse Man

neous assumptions about me. There was still some of that northern/southern dichotomy among students that kept many of us from trusting each other enough to drop our defenses. By this time, I thought of myself as neither a Northerner or a Southerner. I had now lived long enough in Georgia to view myself as simply one comfortable enough to be in any context and win acceptance. Over time, I was accepted as a regular guy, though my status as a non-athlete, English Literature major and Kappa senior was enough to keep this largely junior contingent at arm's length.

During this semester, the school witnessed a number of companies arriving on campus to look over the class of graduating seniors for the purpose of recruitment. One such team was led by a former student, Robert A. DeLeon, who had become a reporter for *Newsday*, a daily newspaper published on Long Island, New York. DeLeon, before dropping out of Morehouse after his sophomore year because he believed that he had learned as much from college as he was going to learn, had served as editor-in-chief of the 1968 Torch, the college's yearbook. He had been viewed by other students as arrogant, pompous and overly confident. I remember being put off by his worldly manner even though he had arrived at Morehouse from high school from his home town of Augusta, Georgia at the age of 15 or 16. Yet, after a while I found his manner tolerable, even amusing, and we became friends.

It turned out that there were grounds for his enormous self-esteem. At the time, Bill Moyers was editor-in-chief of *Newsday* and was so impressed with DeLeon's abilities that he had the paper send him and the managing editor to campus to find out if Morehouse had any more like him. With all of his courtly mannerisms intact, he came to conduct interviews to determine whether any of us, Spelman seniors as well, had any interest in working for his paper. I remember thinking that no matter how successful Robert had become, he had not forgotten us.

The interview was to be held in a group luncheon at Paschal's. Approximately 12 of us, all of the graduating English majors from both colleges (*Newsday* was not interested in recruiting from any of the other schools) were present. At the time there were no journalism courses being taught on any campus at the Atlanta University Center, thus the writers, if any existed at all, were believed to reside in the English department. The occasion was delightful, yet somewhat nerve-racking. Here we all were, sitting around a table, trying as best we could to market ourselves. This was probably our first experience competing directly with each other for employment in our possible life's work and not just for another grade. Everyone was attempting to offer some clever observation or at least a quick and knowledgeable response to general questions put by Robert and his colleague to no one in particular.

It was a competition for which Morehouse's formal as well as informal training was designed to prepare. Almost daily, there would be conducted noisy, impromptu debates among students on one subject or another. On many such occasions, the one who prevailed was the one who could talk loudest, longest and remained focused. Yet, most often these arguments would be won by the one who could employ the most penetrating logic and capture the imagination of those standing around and the successful proponent would then receive the cheers of approval from his classmates.

The Making of a Morehouse Man

After about an hour-and-a-half at luncheon, some students began suggesting that they should return to classes. The interviewers seemed to welcome this, as they thanked all of us for coming and wished us well. As I began to leave, Robert asked me if I had to rush off. I thought he simply wanted to catch up on old times. Since I had no commitments that afternoon, I welcomed the opportunity to chat with him on a one-on-one basis. After the bill was paid, the three of us adjourned to their hotel suite. By now, Robert had cultivated a taste for scotch and offered me one. He must have been no older than nineteen years old, but here he was, my junior, an accomplished professional, offering me a drink. While preparing it, his colleague asked me if I would like to come to New York City. As if on cue, Robert turned around and said that they would like me to consider working for *Newsday*. I was flabbergasted, shocked, excited, delighted and could not believe my ears. Without thinking about it, I agreed to travel to New York.

Later that evening, I was asked by some of those who attended the luncheon if anything was said to me after they had left. A couple of them saw that I had been asked to stay. Word traveled to the others. I felt a little embarrassed when I realized that I was the only one to whom a job offer was made. I thought that I would not say anything to anyone for fear that my gloating would be too pronounced. But alas, my ego overpowered my superego and I excitedly blurted out that I was offered the job. To my surprise and relief, they congratulated me and seemed genuinely pleased that one of us had been made an offer. At least now, one of the irons in my fire was hot.

Above Our Heads

3

19 Feb 69

Dear Folks,

 I imagine by now that you realize that I don't particularly like to write. But perhaps you don't know the reason for this. I just can't stand to write about nothing. In other words when I write to you or anyone else I want to be able to say a little more than "How are you?" or "How's the weather there? It's fine here!"
 Yet, then too, I often do write letters of a superficial type but I try to always incorporate some different or interesting news in them.
 I have been offered a job, either part-time or full-time, as a reporter for a New York (Long Island) newspaper, entitled Newsday, after graduation. Starting salary $8,000. I will be going toNew York on Feb. 26th to spend the weekend at the expense of the newspaper. The trip is designed to determine whether or not I want to accept the job after graduation.
 I have completed the admission requirements for law schools and I am now impatiently waiting for replies.
 Tomorrow I will talk to an additional law school representative - Yale. I have nothing to lose!
 The same time that I mailed this letter I sent for an application to a summer session at the North Carolina College Duke University Institute in Law. This program is designed to see whether or not the prospective law school student really desires to enter law school. The program lasts 8 weeks and if accepted all expenses are paid.
 In the last letter that you sent, was money enclosed? The last amount of money I received was in the sum of

The Making of a Morehouse Man

$45.00. You mentioned about money to pay my phone bill. Was this to what you were making reference? The number here is 523-1830. Area code is 404.

Each day here seems completely different. Unfortunately I believe that it is my extreme moody nature which makes it this way. As a result of my changing moods my actions change. Some days I'm industrious when other days, I am extremely non-productive. I was at first able to cope with this instability but now I know that if I don't change I may await an unhappy destiny. Of course I could rationalize the situation by saying everything happens for the best but that would be too easy. I would like to believe that I am the master of my fate and captain of my ship rather than to accept the doctrines of Calvin.

At any rate I believe somewhat that my outlook becomes more and more optimistic though it is a gradual increase.

About that job, I can arrange it so that I work only for the summer and then go to law school if I still desire to do so. On the other hand, I may attempt to go to Columbia Law and work at the newspaper part-time, such as a friend of mine already employed there is doing.

Look on the bookshelf in Wilkie's room among my college catalogues and see if there is an application for Columbia U. Law School. If so mail it to me please. I imagine things will work out. I haven't been thinking too seriously of the Peace Corps yet the thought still remains vaguely in the back of my mind.

Andrea is all right. As the days go by I see myself more and more unsure of wanting to marry her whereas before I felt that was my only course of action. Don't worry I am in control (I think).

          Love,
          Spencer

Above Our Heads

This was my first trip to New York City and I was so excited I could barely contain myself. I was met at the airport by Bob DeLeon who was there not simply to collect me but was on assignment covering a possible airline strike. This was my first time witnessing an investigative reporter on the job. We were in and out after he followed up on some leads from his editor. We then proceeded to Robert's Manhattan apartment on W. 46th Street. At this time in New York City, one could still park on the streets of midtown without too much difficulty. We then walked the block or so to his third floor walk-up that was situated above an Italian restaurant. He had a small but totally adequate one bedroom apartment that had what I was to learn was an unusual luxury: a rooftop terrace. His apartment was two-thirds the length of the building. The remaining one-third was the terrace for his exclusive use and had a view overlooking 45th Street. This was too much! I wanted to start work at *Newsday* tomorrow even though I had not been formally offered the job and had three months to graduate.

By now, I had learned that the paper was headquartered in Garden City, Long Island which was within an hour's drive from New York City. To make the commute, DeLeon had purchased a new Oldsmobile Tornado. The man had enormous style. I found it hard to believe that this young guy from Augusta had come so far in what seemed to me to be a short space of time. When I learned years later that he had married Diahann Carroll, it did not surprise me in the least.

Soon after dumping my bags in his living room, DeLeon and I hit the streets of his Manhattan. He took me to places that are only pleasant memories, but one spot stood out grandly. A cabaret called "The Electric Flag" rocked with the New York Latin Salsa that I had earlier learned to appreciate in Atlanta. The folks inside were doing the dances that my New York schoolmates had popularized on campus, so I felt strangely at home in a place I had never before been.

The next day we drove to *Newsday*. Robert explained to me that I would probably be encouraged to live in Nassau County. This did not sound all that attractive. The appeal of this job in New York was that it was not just close to New York City but that I could live in New York City. When we arrived at the offices, I was made to feel welcomed, met Bill Moyers and got a tour of the physical plant. Soon I was seated at a desk and given an examination. I was provided with a hypothetical situation involving the killing of a young girl. My "proctor" instructed me to write a feature article based on the facts that I possessed in a file in front of me. The only newspaper experience that I had gained was through a one-year tenure as a member of my high school newspaper staff. This was four years earlier and I had not been around a news office in all of that time. But, I wanted this job. It took me about two hours to draft the article. When completed, the proctor, who was one of the editors, muttered something about "very imaginative but needs some work in vocabulary." Then he proceeded to recommend that I be hired.

Later that evening I was invited to a party for a retiring member of the news staff. As he was leaving, I was being welcomed aboard. It was quite a festive event complete with a company-supplied bar and exquisite seafood that was reportedly a special order from Maine.

Above Our Heads

The people at *Newsday* were truly warm and accepting. I believed that I would enjoy working with them. One reporter in particular befriended me. His name escapes me but I will never forget that his hands were deformed causing him to have to type as I do, using a finger from each hand. Yet, unlike me, he was so fierce on a typewriter, that his hands seemed a blur when he was working. He had been a reporter from the Boston Globe and received an unsolicited offer to work in Garden City. As we got to know each other during my brief stay I discovered that he liked jazz as did I. It happened that while I was in town Lee Morgan was playing at the Blue Note. He volunteered to drive us into the city that night

If I had not been hooked on New York City before that night, I was following it. The Blue Note was and is a venerated jazz venue, drawing only the most notable jazz artists. The location was different from its current room on West 3rd Street, though it was always in the village. I remember that the stage ran the width of the space in the rear. Patrons seated themselves at tables randomly placed, unlike the dense, rigid arrangement that exists today. Here was this Black youngster from Illinois by way of Georgia sitting with the Jewish fellow from New York by way of Boston having a ball. Lee Morgan's "Sidewinder," which I first heard in my freshman year at Morehouse, was still a popular tune, and he was on the stage that night playing it for all that it was worth. I forgot momentarily how freezing cold it was outside, resolving that I would be in NewYork City as soon after graduation as was humanly possible.

I returned from the trip exceptionally proud that all the academic and social training provided me by the college had paid off.

The Making of a Morehouse Man

The people that I met associated with the paper liked me and were excited about my joining with them. I saw my girlfriend that evening at a Morehouse dance. It was the perfect time and place in which to share my experience of the trip. My girlfriend at the time, Andrea, also from Chicago, seemed happy for me. I imagined that she began to wonder where she fit into this picture. I began to think about this myself in earnest.

She was nearing completion of her freshman year at Spelman. I strongly believed that she was entertaining hopes of our getting married upon my graduation. My prospects of becoming a good provider were improving with each passing day. Yet, after seeing life in the Big Apple, my tender years needed more nurturing as a single person. I simply did not want to go to this fascinating metropolis, in a job that I really did not know, with a person about whom I was becoming increasingly uncertain. It was my time to see a new facet of the world. After all, I reasoned, was not education important enough to her to stay at Spelman and complete her studies? I felt the pressure increase to make my intentions known as to how I saw her in my future. What an uncomfortable place to find oneself, especially when other parts of life looked so promising. I began to understand now this Morehouse/Spelman and Meharry/Fisk thing in a new way: as a context for initiating families, with the education of the female as a marvelous byproduct, but holding second place to meeting and marrying. These feelings were to intensify as time continued.

Above Our Heads

4

16 Mar 69

Dear Folks,

 The trip was a huge success. I will report to the job (if I am still interested) on June 10, 1969. Salary: $147.50/week or a little over 8,000 yearly. They really want me for permanent employment. If not accepted in law school this possibility remains.
 I don't understand about the U. of Iowa info. I know I sent in all necessary information. Please check with your friend in office again. I believe an error has been made somewhere. If still no application turns up tell office to send a second one for me to fill. As graduation time nears I become more and more frightened - not fear of not being able to graduate but of having to spend time in a wartime situation which I cannot believe in and which is truly useless. I would hate to defect. Was considering (but not seriously) attending McGill University in Montreal and denouncing American citizenship. Must think more. I know it sounds rash but I'm also somewhat certain that you cannot possibly fathom the pressure of these last few months. This must be the worst psychological year I have ever experienced. I'm sorry to say that Andrea really doesn't help. Chalk up to experience! I'll be glad when I leave but I really can't say the future is bright. In fact, I may wish for these years all over again.
 Did get two letters and money. Address of summer job:
   South Chicago Community Center
   9135 So. Brandon Avenue
   Chicago, Illinois

The Making of a Morehouse Man

Had planned to go to St Petersburg, Florida with income tax return. Looks like I'll be here for break which starts Thursday 19th. I'll write soon.

Love,
Spencer

The income tax return arrived in time for me to enjoy spring break in Tampa/St. Pete. My good friend and fraternity brother Victor Wright and I drove down to Florida in his MGB. It was a relief to get away from the pressure I was feeling from Andrea. I almost let my feelings of guilt about the way I was beginning to feel towards her prevent me from going. After a good "talking to" by Victor, we headed south with about $3.00 between us and Victor's aunt contributed a tank of gasoline for the drive.

Victor's father had most of his family still located in Florida. We were able to stay in a house owned by one of them and were given a private suite. I loved these people and they seemed to love me. It was always to be my experience with the families of other Morehouse men that I would meet that I would be received like another member of the family. The Wrights were educators. Victor's mother began her career as an instructor at Bethune-Cookman College in Daytona Beach, Florida. After coming out of the army in World War II as a captain, Lowry Wright, Victor's father, was appointed business manager at Bethune-Cookman by the college's founder, Mary McLeod Bethune. Vic's Aunt Johnnie Ruth held a doctorate in education and was dean of students at Gibbs Junior College in St. Petersburg. They were a well-respected and widely-known family in this part of Florida and their notoriety gave me immediate entry into the social swirl of that community.

On our first day of driving about the town, specifically the Black section of St. Petersburg, we ran into the Downing sisters. They had known Victor from his previous visits and immediately wanted to engage us in starting our spring break activities, whatever they were to be. Evelyn and Diedre were the daughters of a successful businessman. Their mother was a housewife with no need to work outside of the home, as they were fairly well-to-do. Both Diedre and Evelyn attended the University of Colorado in Denver and had just returned home the day before we arrived. All four of us hit it off instantly and they invited us to their parents' home for luncheon.

Everyone who knew these young women liked them and they seemed to know everyone. I indicated to Victor that we need not hang out with any others as long as we could be with Evelyn and Diedre. Being with them would enable us to meet so many others and therefore increase our fun quota. He agreed. Soon, we found that Diedre was gravitating towards Victor and I was decidedly interested in Evelyn. In all fairness, we liked each other at first sight and I instantly regretted having a serious relationship in Atlanta.

The remaining four days were spent in night after night of house parties: the Downings, the Davises, the Alsups and the Ayers, all connected to one another and all part of the Black elite of St. Petersburg. My last college spring break proved to be the best of the four, eclipsing by leap and bounds the previous one in Florida three years earlier. Evelyn captured my heart and without

The Making of a Morehouse Man

me telling her, she knew it. This was the first woman whom I sang with out loud, unashamedly, and found genuine enjoyment in it. The four of us were inseparable during that week and people loved seeing us all together, enjoying one another so much. Though 21, we were considered good boys from good homes and getting ready to graduate from Morehouse. I was going to be a newspaperman in New York City and Victor was headed to business school.

It was clear that the doors that opened for us were largely due to the fact that we were Morehouse men. We had no money at all and had not begun a working life, yet we were accorded all the respect and hospitality of accomplished men of letters. The generosity and kindness of those families more than sustained our economically-challenged status on that trip. As I look at it now, those people who hosted us were making an investment, not just in us, but in the race. For we were Morehouse men and as such there was the expectation that we were going to rise to prominence in this society and bring others along with us.

5

31 March 69

Dear Folks,

    I went to St. Petersburg, Florida over the break (Mar 19 - 26). It cost me about $10.00, which I had.
    Rec'd money last Friday. Will have this coming Friday and the following Monday out for Easter. Sent in application to Columbia. Enclosed is financial aid sheet for Columbia. Fill it out and send it directly to them:

    School of Law Admissions Office
    Columbia University
    435 West 116th Street
New York, New York 10027

I am now making up course in Shakespeare. No restriction on number of guests for graduation.

As of yet no schedule of activities has been posted. Will keep in touch.

                                Love,
                                Spencer

The student-led confrontation and "lock up" of the members of the Morehouse Board of Trustees was perhaps the single most significant event to occur at Morehouse from 1965 to 1969. The following "Chronology of Events," which was drafted and distributed to the entire student body immediately after this momentous episode in Morehouse's life occurred, sum-

The Making of a Morehouse Man

marizes what happened during the course of one week in April, 1969. The author, while unknown, appeared to have written this eyewitness account as though he had expectations it would be published years after the immediacy of the event had passed.

A CHRONOLOGY OF EVENTS

Sunday, April 13, 1969: Following a debate between Sociology professor Abdul Hakimu (Gerald McWhorter) and Dr. Ralph Lee, Dean of Morehouse College, a group of concerned students met to discuss later meetings with the various [colleges] Boards of Trustees. The purpose of this meeting was to take positive and significant steps toward improving the Atlanta University Center. The initial move came from Morehouse students, and they constituted a majority of those who met. Among the number also were students from Spelman, Clark, and Morris Brown. The interests of the concerned students were: that in these times it is improper for Black schools to be named after obscure white persons; that the separate colleges in the A. U. Center probably could not celebrate a second centennial as small independent colleges; that the colleges should undergo fundamental changes, in terms of their function and how they relate to the surrounding black community; that at least a majority of the Boards of Trustee members controlling Black institutions should be black; that students should participate in the decision-making processes which govern their lives; and that more and better

Above Our Heads

Black curriculum is needed.

It was decided that a letter be drafted to the Boards of Trustees, requesting a meeting with them about the stated issues. It was felt furthermore, that the demands be minimal and just and would receive the approval of the A. U. Center student community.

Wednesday, April 16, 1969 - 12:15p.m.: A group of students submitted a resignation statement to the Board of Trustees; no one resigned.

8:00p.m.: A rally was held in Sale Hall at Morehouse College which was attended by more than 300 students. There were faculty, students, and community spokesmen who addressed the idea of creating one Black university, to be named after Dr. Martin Luther King, Jr. The overwhelming response was in favor of such a program. An effigy was burned outside the main gate of the college representing the old idea of small competing colleges. From there students marched around to the other campuses, singing and shouting slogans.

Meanwhile, eight students (Calvin Butts, Cecil Brim, Carthur Drake, John Jones, William McFarlin, Abraham Marshall, Harold McKelton, and Julius Stevens) met in the Canterbury House where they decided to submit to the Morehouse President of the S.G.A. [Student Government Association] a statement expressing support of the name change of the A.U.Center to the Martin Luther King University Center. A number of reasons were given as basis for the support, but primarily were the following:
(1) Martin Luther King, Jr. is one of the College's most illustrious alumni, (2) as a Black school, we reserve the

right to honor Black heroes, rather than white missionaries, and (3) Martin Luther King, Jr. was a symbol of unity, and this unity should be reflected in the unity of the schools in the center.

Thursday, April 17, 1969 - 10:30a.m.: Nelson Taylor, President of the Morehouse S.G.A., called a meeting of the student body, at which time he presented the idea of changing the name for the reasons stated by those who met the night before in the Canterbury House. The vote was in favor of this idea.

At 2:00p.m. of the same day, a rally was held on the steps of Harkness Hall, the administration building. Students were there to meet with the [Morehouse] Board of Trustees. The Board did not come down, but several students then arranged a meeting for Friday, April 18 at 9:00a.m. with the Board.

That night a meeting was held with representative students from the various campuses and the community at which time student proposals were decided upon and Abdul Hakimu was asked to act as chief negotiator.

A second rally was scheduled at 8:30, the next morning on the steps of Harkness Hall. Friday, April 18, 8:30 a.m.: The assembly on the steps of the building increased by 9:00 a.m., when the representatives from the various campuses and the negotiators met in the suite (room 307) of Harkness Hall.

At approximately 9:30 a.m. the crowd moved upstairs to the third floor where negotiators were meeting. The people in the hall were singing. Between 10:00 a.m. and 10:30 a.m. the crowd dwindled to slightly below 100. The trustee members made an attempt to leave the meeting room before a decision was reached on the proposals before them. This attempt was thwarted by those in the rally who sat at the doors and refused to move. Moving spontaneously, several Morehouse students obtained chains. By 10:45 a.m., both of the third floor exits were locked by chains and secured with padlocks. The elevator was locked also. At this time the trustees began to realize that either the brief, but comprehensive demands were [going to be] deliberated to a mutually agreeable settlement, or they would be detained.

Saturday, April 19, 1969: The Board began deliberations early. The trustees were undecided on whether or not they would meet with students. T.M. Alexander, a member of the Board, said that he definitely would not attend the 10:00 a.m. meeting with the students.

The Morehouse students on the outside of Harkness became angry at not having had the Trustees delivered to them. They held meetings in Sale Hall to discuss the incidents which were occurring. Their number was increased by students, alumni, and faculty, who were against holding the trustees inside. Although force was suggested for freeing the Board members, it was not employed.

At approximately 1:30 p.m., the Board and the concerned students came to an agreement and soon departed.

Brothers and Sisters, this means to us that:

    A. Before these resolutions were passed, the

Morehouse Board had a majority of white trustee members. Now the Morehouse Board will have a majority of Black people.

B. Previously, the white-dominated Board was answerable only to itself, often installing board members for 20 or 30 years. Now they can serve no more than 6 consecutive years, meaning that the composition of the Morehouse Board will reflect the times.

C. Students for the first time have real and equitable power to determine the destiny of their institutions.

D. The Morehouse Board officially voted to support the consolidation of the six institutions if it proves beneficial to the group collectively.

HARAMBEE!

Let Us Pull Together!

The college, its alumni and students, owe a great deal of gratitude for the courage displayed by the eight Morehouse Men who led the charge to change the arcane, paternalistic practices of the school's board of trustees. Butts, McFarlin and Stevens were all members of Kappa; Brim was an Alpha and Marshall was a Sigma. These men demonstrated to the whole community that fraternity men were capable of championing critical issues and were willing to risk their academic lives for the larger good.

All of them suffered some repercussions, short of expulsion. Nelson Taylor, the S.G.A. President during this time and a graduating senior, sided with the protestors and for his part, stayed an additional year to "correct" a "deficiency" in his transcript. Besides being a Kappa, Taylor, ironically, held the honored distinction of being a 1967-68 Merrill Scholar, which meant that because of his academic prowess he earned a junior year abroad, studying at the University of Vienna. This honor also meant that his junior year actually turned out being a fifth year, as these men would return to complete a junior and senior year at Morehouse. Because Nelson was penalized, he ended up staying at Morehouse for six years.

The trustee lock-out is the single most frequently recalled event by Morehouse men who were in attendance during this era. It forever changed the school from being an institution that prepared men for life in the world into a place that created critical thinkers who would reshape the world.

Graduation arrived for me four years after I entered college, a remarkable achievement, given the amount of land mines that littered the course of that journey. In the wee hours of the morning before the Morehouse graduation exercises, Pi chapter of Kappa Alpha Psi held its annual Dawn Dance. Before integration was the law of the land, when Black people wanted to give an elegant affair, there were but two places that came to mind: the Waluhaje Hotel on Westlake Boulevard and the Magnolia Ballroom. Even after Black people could patronize white establishments, socially-conscious Black folk continued to support these establishments.

Though its frame building was not as impressive as the brick structure which housed the Waluhaje, The Magnolia was the perennial favorite primarily because its Vine City location was in close proximity to the school. The Magnolia was located on

The Making of a Morehouse Man

Magnolia Street between Sunset and Vine Streets, but in no way resembled the Sunset and Vine Street of Hollywood. Vine City was one of the toughest Black neighborhoods in Atlanta and yet, that fact notwithstanding, Martin Luther King, Jr. and his family lived in a house on Sunset near two other prominent Black Atlanta families, the Toomers and the Martins, headed by men who were executives associated with the Atlanta Life Insurance Company. Everyone else in Vine City was profoundly impoverished. This enclave of three solidly middle class families all understood the importance of the people who lived around them. They were the same people whose rights Martin championed on a daily basis. They were the same people who had bought burial policies from Atlanta Life for so long that it became a leading insurance company in Black America. They were not leaving Vine City. They had each other and Vine City had them.

The Dawn Dance began at 2 a.m. and did not end until 6 o'clock that morning, plenty of time to drag yourself back to the campus, shower, shave and prepare for graduation. No one dared go to sleep for fear of missing the most important day of one's life. Though I was connected to the fraternity all four years of my college career, I had only heard about the Dawn Dances, preferring to start my summer vacation as soon as classes ended, rather than hanging around campus simply to attend a party. This time it was different. I was celebrating with my classmates and friends the struggles of four, or in the case of some, five years of regimented learning.

The dance was by invitation only. This enhanced its position as the stellar social event of the year. Of course, the fraternity paid for the complete bar and whatever cuisine was served. Though one had a good time attending, it was still very unusual for any of us to come to a party beginning at 2 o'clock in the morning and party until the sun rose. This type of staying up all night was reserved for cram sessions before finals. Nevertheless, there was a high level of energy at the Magnolia for everyone because we knew that in less than 12 hours, we would be newly-minted Morehouse graduates. Yet, my graduating chapter brothers, James Hawes, Jimmie Millhouse, Victor Wright, Karl Merritt and I, were ecstatic. We were being toasted by alumni brothers who always attended the dance to congratulate the new graduates. Yet, because of the time of day this event took place, the Dawn Dance is a blur in most attendees' memories. One thing that did not get lost was how amazing it was to emerge from the ballroom after the party ended and be blinded by the sunlight, evidence that we had partied way past 6 a.m.

Graduation was the first time any of my family had visited Morehouse. It was a good opportunity for them to see the school in its finest hour. Our graduating class was 116 strong and if one had never seen this many Black men gathered in one place wearing academic gowns and graduating from an institution of higher learning, one's breath might get caught in one's throat. My parents were properly impressed. On this occasion my grandmother was in attendance and she was prouder of this moment than even I. For it was she that got me to thinking about attending and here I was four years later, graduating. When we were at the baccalaureate exercises in Spelman's Sisters Chapel, my grandmother could not keep her eyes off me and was smiling so hard and long that if it had been anyone else, I would have thought that they were trying to keep from riotously laughing out loud.

The Making of a Morehouse Man

At the graduation ceremony held in the gymnasium of Samuel H. Archer Hall, I was seated next to my classmate, Henry Gore. It became a bit embarrassing after a while. During the announcements of awards bestowed upon seniors, Gore must have been cited at least five times. When this would occur every eye in the room would turn to acknowledge him. While they could easily see who was receiving the award, as he would stand each time his name was called, they also could see who was not going to receive any award...me.

After the ceremony and the photo ops subsided, people began bidding farewell to class mates. I had arranged to fly back to Chicago to avoid the reindoctrination car ride back into my parents' home. So after seeing them off, along with my brothers Marvin and Billy and other family members, I deposited my cap and gown with the custodian and went for a walk around the old school one more time. My flight was not to depart for a few hours more, so I took some time to reflect on my experiences. I walked to the steps of Harkness Hall and sat. I thought about all of the events that had taken place in this venerable spot: the Freshman Class photo, the King funeral, the trustees' lockout, just to name a few. I reminisced about standing in long lines that often spilled out unto these very steps, with students attempting to pay a bill, collect mail or check on academic credits.

As I sat there pondering the past, thinking of all those days spent growing in this place, most of the dreadful memories were pushed out of the way by rosy flashbacks. They had the effect of causing me not to want to leave: the good and caring teachers, my fraternity and its gift for making heavy times light, the diversity of Black people that I truly discovered here and my appreciation for it. This, indeed was a "splendid school," a "pleasant place" that had changed my life forever.

A panorama of options lay before me, which included job offers and professional school acceptance letters. Morehouse had helped all of us to see the possibilities that lay ahead. The next steps I would take would lead me to the best time of my life.

Epilogue

Morehouse today is a very different place than it was 30 years ago when I graduated. I applaud the changes. It has become a national college with students from every state in the Union. Instead of playing football games in the "dustbowl" of Herndon Stadium of Morris Brown College, Morehouse has its own stadium. Named in honor of Chemistry department chairman Professor Burwell T. Harvey who coached winning basketball and football teams at Morehouse from 1916 to 1929, the arena is a fitting complement to the explosion of physical development that the college has witnessed largely in the last 25 years.

The continuing record of achievement of the College's graduates exceeded, I am certain, even Benjamin Mays' demanding expectations. The United States Congress now has three Morehouse Men serving in its chambers: Sanford D. Bishop '68, Earl Hilliard '64 and Major Owens '56, all first elected within the last one and a half decades, the earliest being Owens who was sent to Congress in 1983. Today, her graduates number more than 12,000. In 1969, the year that I graduated, one was hard-pressed to name 10 living alumni with national prominence. During my years alone, the college produced such giants as Charles Allen '70, president and CEO of First Independence National Bank of Detroit; Julian H. Bond '71, chairman of the NAACP; Calvin Butts '71, pastor of New York City's Abyssinia Baptist Church and president of the State University of New York at Old Westbury; Herman Cain '67, CEO of Godfather Pizza; Robert C.

Above Our Heads

Davidson '67, chairman and CEO of Surface Protection Industries; Sidney Harris '71, the first African-American dean of the College of Business Administration at Georgia State University; M. William Howard '67, president of New York Theological Seminary; Samuel L. Jackson '71, film star and Oscar nominee; Howard F. Jeter, U.S. Ambassador; Michael Lomax '68, president of Dillard University; C. Vernon Mason '67, noted former civil rights attorney and Baptist minister; Roderic Pettigrew '72, physician and nuclear physicist; Thomas G. Sampson '68, managing partner of the oldest and largest African-American law firm in the state of Georgia; Maceo Sloan '71, financier and CEO of Sloan Financial Group and chairman of NCM Capital Management Group; Roy Terry '66 and Rudolph Terry '69, president and executive vice-president of Terry Manufacturing Company; and Edward L. Wheeler '69, president of United Theological Seminary, Ohio.

When looking beyond the short span of time represented by my years at Morehouse, other generations produced enormous leaders too numerous to mention. Yet, I would be remiss if I did not attempt a short list of persons who made their marks upon this nation in a variety of professions. Besides the three Martin Luther Kings (Sr. '30, Jr. '48 and III '79), Donn Clendenon '56, New York Mets outfielder and 1969 World Series MVP; Samuel Dubois Cook '48, former president of Dillard University; Abraham Davis '61, author and professor of political science; George W. Haley '49, U.S. Ambassador to The Gambia; Maynard H. Jackson '56; Spike Lee '79, the film director; Edwin Moses '78, the Olympic track star; Louis Sullivan '54, former White House Cabinet member; Mordecai Johnson '11, a past president of Howard University; James M. Nabrit, Jr. '23, another past president of Howard; Samuel M. Nabrit '25, a past president of Texas Southern University; Bill Nunn III '76, film star; Lerone Bennet '49, managing editor of *Ebony* magazine; David Satcher '63, Surgeon General of the United States; Howard Thurman '23, theologian and religious mystic; Nima A. Warfield '94, first African American Rhodes Scholar from a historically Black college; Robert M. Franklin '75, President of the Interdenominational Theological Center; Edward C. Mazique '33, a past president of the National Medical Association; Walter E. Massey '58, president of Morehouse College; John W. Davis '11, a past president of West Virginia State College; Richard I. McKinney '31, former president of Storer College and chairman of the philosophy department at Morgan State University; and R. Roosevelt Thomas '66, member of the Morehouse College faculty and perhaps the leading authority on diversity in the workplace. All have been men of unquestionably enormous accomplishment.

 The three guys with whom I was initiated into Kappa went on to achieve greatly in their chosen vocations. James Hawes '69, became CEO of a communications company after serving as CEO of the Philadelphia Gas and Light Company and CEO of US West Communications' Nebraska Operation. Karl Merritt '69, became a career naval officer. Donald Hense '70, served as Vice-President of Development for the National Urban League.

 The graduates of Morehouse College, in an overwhelming number of instances, have excelled in life, setting a standard of achievement for men and women just beginning their work lives to emulate. Notwithstanding the impressive and dramatic changes which the institution has undergone in the last three decades, Morehouse continues to carry out its mission of building men. And just like the words of the Morehouse College Hymn intone, her graduates are grateful:

> "True forever, true forever
> to old Morehouse may we be
> So to bind each son the other
> into ties more brotherly."

Index for ABOVE OUR HEADS

A Candle in the Dark, 5
Abercrombie & Fitch, 52
Abernathy, Ralph, 181, 186, 187
Alabama, 10, 22
Alaska, 11, 37
    Bethel, 37
Allen, Richard, 163
Alpha Phi Alpha, 45, 46, 69, 105, 135, 196
    Sphinx, 46
American Baptist Home Mission Society, 2, 3
Antioch, 93
Aquascutum, 52
Archer Hall, Samuel H., 197
Armstead, Ralph, 90
Atlanta Life Insurance Company, 233
Atlanta Police Dept., 23
Atlanta University, 13, 20, 29, 75, 114, 158, 174, 177
    Harkness Hall, 186, 187, 229, 235
    Trevor Arnett Library, 74-76
Atlanta University Center (AUC), 13, 39, 40, 65, 133, 167, 173, 214, 227
Auburn Avenue,186
Augusta Institute, 2
Baldon, Billy, 67, 73
    Mrs. Baldon, 73
"Bang, Bang," 164

Bataan, Joe, 164
Beat Generation, 31
Beatles, The, 201
Beech, Malcolm, 173, 174, 183, 184
Belafonte, Harry, 186
Bennet Hall, 131, 133, 134, 153, 173
Bethune-Cookman, 91, 223
Bethune, Mary McLeod, 223
Bevel, James, 181, 186
Bishop, Sanford, 71, 77
Black Atlanta, 85
Blake, Mavis, 40
Block Boys, 167
Blue Note, The, 220
Board of Trustees, 132, 226, 229
    AUC colleges' Boards of Trustees, 227, 228
Bowman, Carl, 135
Bravo, Sonny, 164
Brazeal, Dean Brailsford Reese, 25, 26
Breckinridge House, 96, 97
    John Cabell Breckenridge, 96
Brim, Cecil, 228, 231
Brooks Brothers, 52
Brooks, Sidney, 163
Brown, James, 201
Burt, Larry, 106, 155, 156
Burton, Elias, 163
Butler, Jerry, 44

Butts, Calvin, 228, 231
Byoune, Granny, 48, 74
Byoune, Loleta, 33
Byoune, Wilkie, 33, 36
Cabbage, Charles, 71, 124
California, 10, 96, 181
Campbell, Finley, 103, 106-108
Canterbury House, 29, 30, 31, 59, 76, 173, 177, 228
Carmichael, Stokely, 129, 181, 186
Carnegie Public Library, 74
Chestnut Street, 22
Chevalir, Roland, 174
Chicago, Ill, 8, 10, 11, 49, 51, 61, 62, 106, 113
    University of, 15, 129
Chisholm, Shirley, 181
Chivers, Naomi, 108
Chivers, Walter, 103, 108
Chivers Dining Room, 157
Christmas, 113, 114, 125
Cintron, Wigberto, 163
Citizens Trust Bank, 60, 67
Claflin, v
Clark College, 12, 21, 29, 66, 114, 158, 167, 168, 177, 227
Clark University, 129
Clark, Michael, 163
Collier, Lewis, 163
Columbia University, 25
    Law school, 217, 226
Committee on College Literary Magazines, 143
Crabs, 12, 21, 22

Crabgrass, 104
Cross, Robert, 8, 9, 28, 38
    family of, 118
Cuba, Joe, 164
Dancy, Walter, 30, 34
Dash, Hugh, 96
Davis, Michael T., 163
Davis, Miles, 25, 178
    Bitches' Brew, 178
Davis, Jr., Sammy, 186
DeLeon, Robert, 213, 218
    marriage to Dianne Carroll, 218
DeVerges, Ronald, 200
Dillard, Morris, 103, 108
Dillard University, v
Downings, 224
    Diedre, 224
    Evelyn, 224
Drake, Carthur, 228
Dump, 90, 91
Dunn, John, 56
Ebenezer Baptist Church, 186
Electric Flag, The, 219
Emory University, 147
    Newman House, 158
Episcopal Church, 27, 29
Essence magazine, 4
Ethridge, Samuel, 30
Faulkner, 64
Fair Street, 19
Fania All-Stars, 164
Fannin, James, 163
Fisk University, v, 40, 42- 44, 138, 190

Florida, 10
    Daytona Beach, Fla., 91
    Ft. Lauderdale, Fla., 90
    Orlando, Fla., 90
Florida A&M University, 42, 43, 45
Fort Valley, Ga., 28
Founder's Day, 119, 132
Franks, John T., 163
Freshman Week, 13, 17
Friendship Baptist Church, 3, 96
Gaither, Edmund Barry, 27, 30, 31
Garcia, Robert, 163
Gary, Howard V., 163
Georgia, 10, 22
    Augusta, Ga, 2, 96
    Camilla, Ga, 111
    Columbus, 132, 133, 142, 146-148
    Rome, 134, 135
Georgia State College, iii
Georgia Tech, 147
Ghana, Accra, 203
Gholdston, Robert, 10, 96
Gibbs, Dr. William C., 132
Gilbert, Billy, 10, 77, 82
Glee Club, 27
Glore, Byron, 83, 84
Gloster, Hugh M., iv
Grady Hospital, 37
Graham, Fr., 171, 175, 189
Graves Hall, 187
Gray, James, 71
Greek show, 99, 100

Greene, Lambert, 163
Grisham, Clarence, 163
Groove Phi Groove, 96
Haines, Coach James, 108, 162-164
Hakimu, Abdul (Gerald McWhorter), 227, 229
Hamer, Fannie Lou, 181
Hampton Institute, 33
Hare, Nathan, 74
Harlem, 11
Harrell, Theodric, 185, 188
Harris, Dottie, 190
Harris, J.B., 189
Harris, Sylvia Ann, 189, 190
Harvey, Il, 67,
Hawes, James, 77, 82, 83, 103, 104, 105, 110, 111, 115, 127, 146-148, 198, 234
Hayes, Isaac, 184
Hell Week, 83, 110
Henderson, Micky, 171, 172, 189
Hendrix, Jimi, 178
    "Are You Experienced?" 178
    "Machine Gun," 178
    "Purple Haze," 178
    "The Wind Cried Mary," 178
Hense, Donald, 34, 111, 114, 115, 127, 196, 198, 209, 211, 212
Hewitt, 144
High Point, N.C., 10

Hill, Mark, 77
Hodge, Haywood, 27, 30, 31
Holmes, Herbert, 203
Homecoming, 119
Hope, John, 3
Houser, John, 135
Howard University, v, 27, 42, 43
Hudlin, Richard, 77
Hume, Jeanette, 21, 55, 67, 71
Humphrey, Hubert H., 186
Hunter Street, 116, 178, 183
Illinois, University of, 68, 180
Indiana University, 68
Interdenominational Theological Center, 13, 133
Inuit, 11
Iron Butterfly, 201
J. Press, 52
Jackson, Duane, 8, 9, 28
    family of, 118
Jackson, Mahalia, 186
Jackson, Samuel L., 24
Jamaica, Queens, NY, 52
James, Milton, 146
James Whitcomb Riley Elementary School, 47
James, Willis Lawrence, 25
Jennings, Samuel, 90
Jeter, Howard, 49
Joe, Isaac, 77
Johnson, Mordecai, v
Johnson, Robert, 126
    Black Entertainment Network [BET], 126
Johnson, Stephen, 52

Johnson, Tobe, 103, 107
Jones, Dr. Edward A., 4
Jones, John, 228
Joyce Street, 202
Kappa Alpha Psi, 46, 67-71, 73, 77, 78, 92, 110, 121, 196
    Chicago Kappa House, 126, 114, 126, 139
    Dawn Dance, 92, 142, 232-234
    Magnolia Ballroom, 232
    Doghouse, 83
    Kappa Conclave, 204, 205
    Kappa Karnival (Southern Illinois University), 180, 181
    Pi Chapter, 70, 71, 78, 113, 116, 126, 142, 174, 188, 232
    St. Louis, 111, 127
    Scrollers Club, 69, 89, 110, 112, 113
    Southeast Province, 142, 146
Kennedy, Robert "Bobby," 186
Kennedy, Edward, 186
Kennedy, John F., 170, 187
Kennedy, Melvin Dow, 61, 62, 65, 128-130
King, Isaiah B., 163
King, Jr., Dr. Martin Luther, v, 2, 24, 30, 129, 141, 228, 229
    assassination of, 181
    funeral of, 185, 187

Martin Luther King, Jr.,
  Blvd, 178
Martin Luther King, Jr.
  University Center, 228
Korean War, 89
Lane, Alvin H., 131, 132
  Alvin H. Lane Dining
    Room, 96
Lanier, Anne, 112
Lee, Ralph, 205
Lewis, Arthur, 30
Lieba, Juan, 71, 163
Lincoln University (Pa.), 93
Long, Edward, 212
Louisville & Nashville Railroad,
  8, 138, 139
Loving Spoonful, The, 178, 179
Mack, Charles, 27, 30, 31
Malcolm X, 30, 141, 181, 183,
  187
Markham, Il, 47
Marshall, Abraham, 228, 231
Martin, Curtis, 67
  son of Vivian and
    Marion, 67
Mason, C. Vernon, 49, 112, 114
Mays, Benjamin E., iii-v, 62, 98,
  186, 196
  home of, 187
Mays Hall, 153, 170, 172, 208,
  211
McFarlin, William, 228, 231
McKelton, Harold, 228
McKenntee, Charles "Sunshine,"
  163

Meharry Medical School, 44,
  138
Merritt, Karl, 111, 114, 115,
  127, 234
Millhouse, Jimmie, 71, 77, 234
Mitchell, Eric, 103, 105, 106
Mitchell, Reginald, 67, 74
  Mrs. Mitchell, 73
Monroe, La., 10
Morehouse, Henry L., 3
Morehouse School of Religion,
  134
Morgan, Lee, 220
  "The Sidewinder," 220
Morris Brown College, 13, 66,
  114, 158, 167, 168, 177, 227
  Herndon Stadium, 213
Music Dept., 25
Muslim, 127
National Collegiate Athletic
  Assn. (NCAA), 163
Nashville, 40, 42, 44- 46
Neff, Samuel H., 103, 106, 108
  of Pomona College, 96,
    108
New Catalyst, The, 142, 143,
  146, 209, 212
  Award, Committee on
    College Literary
    Magazines, 129
Newman House, 170, 173-177,
  179, 185, 188, 202, 203
  at Emory, 175
Newport Jazz Festival, 92
Newsday, 213-216, 219

Bill Moyers, Editor-in-Chief, 213
Garden City location of, 217, 220
New York City, 10, 214, 218-220, 225
Nick, 11, 12, 37, 38
Nix, William, 20
Nixon, Richard M., 186
Nyack, NY, 21
Okeefe, Arthur, 77
Omega Psi Phi, 69, 196
Palmieri, Charlie, 164
Pan Hellenic Council, 196, 207, 208
Parsons, Connie, 34
Paschal's, 183, 214
Paul Stuart, 52
Peace Corps, 195, 203
Phi Beta Sigma, 69, 135, 196
Phi Lambda, 135, 196
Powell, Kenneth, 34
Puente, Tito, 164
Pye, Tommie, 77
Quarles Court, 10, 96, 115, 196
   Units, The, 10
      Unit "5," 10, 11, 96, 196
Quarles, Rev. Frank, 3, 96
Raines, Delano, 77
Randolph-Macon Women's College, 71
Reading Room, The, 68
"Reefer Madness," 165
Reeves, David, 82

Riley Elementary School, James Whitcomb, 52
Robert Hall, 80, 208
Robinson, Neal "Bama," 200
Rockefeller, Laura Spelman, 14
Roman Catholic Church, 156, 158, 171, 173, 188
Ross, Diana, 186
Ruscito, Joseph, 163
Rustin, James, 181
Sale Hall, 228
   Chapel, 107
Salsa, 148, 219
Sam and Dave, 201
Samuel H. Archer Hall, 177, 211
Santayana, George, 56
Scott, Fr. Warren, 29, 30
Selective Service System, 89
Shakespeare, 30
   Iago, 30
   Othello, 30
   The Tempest, 55
Sheffield, Ala., 10
Sisters' Chapel, 234
Smith, Harvey, 141
Smith, John H. "Cochise," 201, 202
Smith, Michelle, 30
Somalia, Mogadishu, 203
Somerville, James, 198-200
Somerville, Joseph, 97, 198, 199
Southern Intercollegiate Athletic Conference, 162
Southern Pacific Railroad Station, 104

Southern University, 33
Spelman College, 12,13
Springfield Baptist Church, 2, 3
Springfield College, 162
Stevens, Julius, 227, 208
Stewart, Ed, 200
Stone, Sly, 161, 181, 201
Student Court, 33, 55, 209
Student Government Assn., 198, 203
Tappan Zee Bridge, 19
Taylor, Nelson, 71, 203, 229, 231, 232
    Merrill Scholar, 232
    student, University of Vienna, 232
Tennessee
    Chattanooga, 60
    Memphis, Tenn., 135
    Nashville, Tenn., 37, 39, 41, 138, 139
Tennessee State University, 42, 43, 45
Terrell, Bob, 143
Thanksgiving, 109, 111, 112
The Loving Spoonful, 161
Thomas, Edgar, 153-155
Thurman, Dr. Howard, v, 5, 24, 131
Tigers, 23
Tigersharks, 162
Tuskeegee, v
Union Station (Chicago), 8, 126
United Church of Christ, 52
"Up South," 12

U.S. Army, 89
U.S. News and World Report, 4
Vietnam War, 30, 72, 89, 139-141, 143
Vine City, 232, 233
Wall Street Journal, The, 4
Waluhaje, 232
Ware, Jefferson T., 117
Warwick, Dionne, 44
Watson, George, 21, 34, 96
Watson, Thomas, 77
Weaver, Reginald, 43, 52, 53, 56
    Danville, Il, 53
Wells, James, 96
West, Robert, 97, 98, 201, 207
"Where the Boys Are," 91
White, Rev. William Jefferson, 2
"Why Do Fools Fall in Love," 113
Wilder, Jr., Samuel, G., 131, 134, 135
Wilkins, Milton, 77
Williams Tavern, 116
Wine Psi Phi, 96
Wright, Lowry, 121, 223
Wright, Pamela, 121
Wright, Paula, 121
Wright, Pauline, 121
Wright, Victor, 121, 122, 189, 190, 223, 234
Xavier, v
Yale University, 71
Yates and Milton, 22, 23
Yokely, Clarence, 10, 96
Young, Andrew, 186